Social Media and Integrated Marketing Communication

Social Media and Integrated Marketing Communication

A Rhetorical Approach

Jeanne M. Persuit

LEXINGTON BOOKS
Lanham • Boulder • New York • Toronto • Plymouth, UK

Published by Lexington Books
A wholly owned subsidiary of The Rowman & Littlefield Publishing Group, Inc.
4501 Forbes Boulevard, Suite 200, Lanham, Maryland 20706
www.rowman.com

10 Thornbury Road, Plymouth PL6 7PP, United Kingdom

British Library Cataloguing in Publication Information Available

Library of Congress Cataloging-in-Publication Data

Library of Congress Cataloging-in-Publication Data Available
ISBN 978-0-7391-7113-4 (cloth)   — ISBN 978-0-7391-7114-1 (electronic)
ISBN 978-1-4985-1616-7 (pbk)

Dedication

This book is dedicated to my husband, Robert,
and my son, John Francis.

Contents

Introduction

I teach an introductory class in Integrated Marketing Communication that is a large (for our campus) lecture class of about seventy. We were discussing social media in IMC in class one day in February, right after the Egyptian uprising that moved President Mubarak out of office and launching the "Arab Spring." I mentioned Kenneth Cole—a designer whose boots I was wearing while teaching and his ill-conceived tweet about the Cairo protests: "Millions are in uproar in #Cairo. Rumor is they heard our new spring collection is now available online at http://bit.ly/KCairo – KC."[1]

The students' reaction (most hadn't heard of his Twitter gaffe) ranged from disbelief to disgust. "What an idiot!" they exclaimed. "Who is this guy?" asked a few. No one applauded his comic timing or wittiness. Then I asked the question: "Will your buying habits change? *Will you stop buying Kenneth Cole designs* because of this tweet?" The students shifted in their seats. Some said "Well, I don't buy it in the first place, so I'm probably not going to start." A few chimed in "I won't buy anything from him anymore." But one student raised her hand and said "Yes, this was stupid, but I don't buy Kenneth Cole shoes because I like him personally or because I follow him on Twitter. He was stupid on an international stage, but I'm not going to boycott him."

The class ended and I cleaned up, mulling the student's comment. How could she put fashion over social justice? How could she so casually dismiss this display of ignorance and superficiality? What was I doing wrong in the classroom to cause this response?

And then I looked at my suede Kenneth Cole boots, with a ruffle up the side and a comfortable heel; I had patiently waited for the boots go

1

on sale to finally purchase. Was I running out to burn my boots in a protest of Kenneth Cole's hubris? No, I wasn't.

This anecdote illustrates a few things. First, I need to curtail my shoe habit. Second, that Kenneth Cole's biggest blunder was thinking his commentary on current events was something his audience wanted to hear. Obviously, they didn't. Kenneth Cole apologized in a tweet, removed the offending tweet, and posted another apology on his Facebook page. At press time, his business was still intact.[2]

My aim for this book is to neither overstate nor undersell the issues that social media present to ethical integrated marketing communication. This book attempts to situate social media as a human communication effort within an organizational context; specifically, how an organization's communication with external audiences can be effective and ethical through social media technology. By approaching this area constructively, engaging the multiple tensions present in any discussion of new technology and its impacts on communication, I am hoping to offer reasonable approaches grounded in Cicero's rhetorical theory that work in this historical moment. Anecdotally, when I mention the topic of this book (social media, IMC, epideictic rhetoric, and rhetorical decorum), responses from academics and practitioners alike range on a continuum: at one end, proclaiming that we've never seen any phenomena that affects communication like social media before, to the other end, which deplores the Millennial generation and its dependence on social media to communicate and which will eventually lead to the end of our world as we know it. Neither end of the spectrum is helpful or accurate, especially when considering technology's impact on the move from oral to literate culture, the concerns of rhetorical decorum that are no less pressing now than they were 2,000 years ago, and the necessity of human communication in the marketplace. It is in these three areas that this book will situate its argument. My hope is that I articulate the argument that while yes, social media *is* a big deal, it is not a big dealbreaker. Twitter does not signal the end of civilization any more than writing ushered in an era of indefensible bad ideas (per Plato). In fact, many of the arguments against technology in communication today are similar in substance, if not in style, to arguments against writing, against the printing press, and against other forms of mass media. While it is not my intent to answer these arguments in this book, I hope to offer historical context for these arguments so that we may learn from them instead of mindlessly repeating them.

Acknowledgments

G.K. Chesterton said, "I would maintain that thanks are the highest form of thought; and that gratitude is happiness doubled by wonder." With this in mind, I would like to thank all of those who helped me throughout the writing of this book.

First, I would like to thank my editor, Alison Northridge, editorial assistant Johnnie Simpson, and former editors Lenore Lautigar and Rebecca McCrory from Lexington Books/Rowman & Littlefield. Your collective patience and assistance has made this a wonderful experience.

Second, my colleagues and students in the Department of Communication Studies at the University of North Carolina Wilmington, especially Dr. Richard K. Olsen, my chair, Dr. Stephen L. Pullum, and Ms. Tammala A. Bulger, deserve my gratitude for their understanding and motivation.

At the Duquesne University Communication Ethics Conference in June 2012, I received extremely helpful feedback from Dr. Gerard A. Hauser and Dr. Ramsey Eric Ramsey that helped propel this book to completion.

I would also like to thank Dr. Ronald C. Arnett, Dr. Calvin L. Troup, Dr. Janie M. Harden Fritz, and Dr. Christina L. McDowell Marinchak for their significant guidance and support. I will never be able to thank them enough, but I won't stop trying!

Without the editing and research assistance of Ms. Lisa Huynh, this book would never have become a reality. She served as sounding board, cheerleader, and enthusiastic reader. She's not only one of my soaring Seahawks—she is a blessing and a friend.

I rely on Chesterton's idea that "gratitude is happiness doubled by wonder" when I thank my whole family, especially my parents, Cissy Bowman and Dan Bowman, my sister, Amy, and my brother, Patrick, for all their love and encouragement.

Finally, my husband, Robert, has been my stabilizing influence for fourteen years. I am blessed to have a partner who understands me the way he does. He and our son, Jake, are my biggest fans, and I am theirs. I thank them for their love and inspiration.

Another aspect of this book is that it concerns social media as part of integrated marketing communication. Studying social media as interpersonal communication, while a very worthwhile pursuit, is not what this project aims to do. When individuals communicate through these channels on behalf of an organization, non-profit, for-profit, publicly or privately held, business-to-consumer (B2C) or business-to-business (B2B), they tweet, update, post, and comment as *the organization*. In the organizational consulting I've done for businesses as they contemplate a social media presence, I've found that leaders in the organizations imagine someone not themselves being the voice of their organization through social media. The illusion that social media presence is free of cost shows the wizard behind the curtain when I ask "and who will be responsible for maintaining your presence?" It may be free to set up a WordPress account, but the responsibility for its maintenance will cost an organization time and effort. The risk inherent in unleashing your own brand through social media may be too much for some organizations to bear. It is my hope that this book will provide some "good reasons"[3] for thoughtful organization leaders to consider if they attempt to establish a presence in social media.

Finally, this book depends on a *praxis* (theory-informed action) approach to IMC and to social media. I offer ancient rhetorical theory—Cicero's theory of rhetorical decorum—as the theory grounding the action of IMC and social media. This is only one of many theoretical directions in which we can go in this area. Some scholars deplore the lack of theory in IMC. I am excited about the possibilities that communication and rhetorical theory can offer the study, teaching, and practice of IMC. My students seem to be excited about it too. It's satisfying to ask "Why?" and receive answers that allow us to connect our everyday practices with the theory in the communication discipline. The rhetorical tradition attends to temporality, locality, particularity, and contingency.[4] Social media and IMC can also be described as temporal, local, particular, and contingent.

In chapter 1, I explain the communicative characteristics of social media and some philosophical ideas that are helpful when considering social media from a communication perspective, including the shift from orality to literacy as described by Walter Ong and Marshall McLuhan, and the relationship between social media's permanent yet ephemeral qualities.

Chapter 2 details a history and philosophy of integrated marketing communication and offers a rhetorical approach to IMC. Chapter 3 explores epideictic rhetoric and rhetorical decorum from a Ciceronian perspective and its implications for postmodernity. Chapter 4 examines the role of the audience in social media and IMC and how audiences and organizations can find common ground in postmodernity. Chapter 5 addresses communication ethics in social media from a virtue ethics perspective, considering issues such as lying versus secrecy, questions of authenticity, and narrative coherence and coordination. This book hopes to offer a praxis approach to social media in IMC: how rhetorical theory can inform ethical action, the role of *phronesis* in social media and IMC, and contemporary examples of *praxis* and *phronesis* in action in social media and IMC.

Notes

1. Brenna Ehrlich, "Kenneth Cole's #Cairo Tweet Angers the Internet," *Mashable* 2011, http://mashable.com/2011/02/03/kenneth-cole-egypt/ (accessed March 6, 2013).

2. "Kenneth Cole Tweet Uses #Cairo to Promote Spring Collection," *The Huffington Post* 2011, http://www.huffingtonpost.com/2011/02/03/kenneth-cole-tweet-uses-c_n_818226.html (accessed March 6, 2013).

3. Walter R. Fisher, *Human Communication as Narration: Toward a Philosophy of Reason, Value, and Action* (Columbia: University of South Carolina Press, 1989), 57.

4. Albert R. Jonsen and Stephen Toulmin, *The Abuse of Casuistry: A History of Moral Reasoning* (Berkeley and Los Angeles: University of California Press, 1990), 74.

Chapter 1
Social Media as Rhetoric and Communication

The interaction with online content may have its early genesis in Usenet, the project of two graduate students from Duke University and one from UNC-Chapel Hill. This message and file exchange program originated in 1979; "Many social aspects of online communication—from emoticons and slang acronyms such as LOL to flame wars—originated or were popularized on Usenet."[1]

In a 2010 article in *Forbes* Magazine,[2] Bercovici states that the first person to coin the term "social media" is actually debatable. First, Tina Sharkey, who owns the domain socialmedia.com and used to work for AOL, has been saying that she was the first to use the term. However, she didn't register for that URL until 1999. Ted Leonsis, another AOL executive, used the term in the way that it is used now back in 1997 (Bercovici supplies this 1997 quotation with his fuse of the word), but Leonsis claims that he's been using the word since the early 1990s. Finally, Darrell Berry argues he started using the word in 1994 when he was working for Matisse.

The growth of these technologies to connect users and content eventually led to what Tim Reilly named "Web 2.0"—the technologies that were marked by the enabling of user-generated content that could be shared with little technical knowledge or hardware investment. Web 2.0 technologies were situated within a network and hosted on servers, fostering an organic categorization of content and interaction between users and content.[3]

We use the term "social media" to encompass a variety of technologies. Clay Shirky describes them as:

> Communication tools that are flexible enough to match our social capabilities, and we are witnessing the rise of new ways of coordinating action that take advantage of that change…we are living in the middle of a remarkable increase in our ability to share, to cooperate with one another, and to take collective action, all outside the framework of traditional institutions and organizations.[4]

Some hallmarks of these technologies are the abilities to publish and comment on content, to establish personal and professional connections, to move what has been in the realm of professionals (like video production or web design) into the hands of non-professionals for business and leisure activities.

Social Media and Media Ecology

Social media is not communication without the human beings who use it as a tool. It is a medium (it's even in the name), and the difference between media and communication is one explored by the study of media ecology. The work of Walter Ong, Neil Postman, Jacques Ellul, Marshall McLuhan, and Lance Strate explores the relationship between media and communication. McLuhan's axiom "the medium is the message" succinctly describes the study of media ecology; according to Strate, "Simply put, it is the idea that the media or technologies that we use play a leading role in how and what we communicate, how we think, feel, and use our senses, and in our social organization, way of life, and world view."[5]

Strate adds that McLuhan's four laws of media (in the form of four questions) can be employed as a heuristic for a new medium: "What does the medium enhance or extend? What does it obsolesce? What does it retrieve that an earlier medium obsolesced? And what does it reverse or flip into when pushed to the extreme?"[6] McLuhan himself did not limit the tetrad to media; the term he uses is "human artefact," and he describes the laws of media as "intended to provide a ready means of identifying the properties of and actions exerted upon ourselves by our technologies and media and artefacts. They do not rest on any concept or theory, but are empirical, and form a practical means of perceiving the action and effects of ordinary human tools and services. They apply to all human artefacts, whether hardware or software, whether bulldozers or buttons, or poetical styles or philosophical systems."[7] We can ask McLuhan's four laws of media questions of social media to provide a hermeneutic entrance—a point at which we can enter the conversation of social media as human communication. McLuhan actually diagrams the responses to the tetrad to emphasize the simultaneity of the effects of the "artefact;" the question are not hierarchical but should be engaged all at once.[8]

The first question, "what does the medium enhance or extend," when applied to social media, returns multiple answers. The medium enhances the mundane events in ordinary lives: doctor's appointments, pet photos, children's first words/steps/days of school/dates, birthday wishes, and funeral condolences. Social media extends the relationships that naturally fade throughout a lifetime, such as school friends, one-time roommates, ex-boyfriends and girlfriends, and former co-workers, by allowing a connection across time and space—windows that put us back into the everyday lives of these people, whose habits and idiosyncrasies used to be so familiar. The medium also extends the presence of an organization into an individual's cyberspace; when I post about my child's first dentist appointment on Facebook, advertisements for pediatric dentists in the Wilmington area pop up to the right of my profile. Because I have an open profile on Twitter, other accounts can begin to follow me without notification. Occasionally, local businesses see my university affiliation and decide to follow me. This is no accident. The algorithms that allow us to search and retrieve pertinent information online are being used by people and organizations to find me and others in my demographic and psychographic profile. I offer these as empirical observations, which, as McLuhan says, encourage us to consider how we use the tools and media and artifacts in our everyday lives.

McLuhan explains the second question of the laws of media, "what does the media obsolesce?" As a result of the response to the first question: "If some aspect of a situation is enlarged or enhanced, simultaneously the old condition or unenhanced situation is displaced thereby. What is pushed aside or obsolesced by the new 'organ'?"[9] One of the old conditions pushed aside by the new organ of social media might be the novelty of connecting with an old friend in a letter, on the phone, or in person. "Friending" someone on Facebook whom you haven't seen in twenty years can be a jarring event, especially when you are given access to this person's cultivated online persona after twenty years of non-communication. My ability to remember birthdays is pitiful; Facebook reminds me of birthdays I once knew or never knew, and all I have to do is post "Happy Birthday" to perform some relationship maintenance. As a professor, I maintain my own rules for online relationships with students (I will not let them be friends on Facebook until after they graduate; following me on Twitter and connecting on LinkedIn are permissible), but these media still give my students access to me that never existed in pre-social media times. Sometimes, this is beneficial; for example, when I'm traveling to a conference I can still keep virtual office hours and respond to questions in a timely manner. However, I find that I am more guarded about my online persona than my students are. What does this mean for the teacher-student relationship. Does this heightened access improve our communication and cultivate trust, or does it violate relationship expectations for both parties? Professors who teach in the areas of IMC, public relations, and social media share these concerns. We should be modeling appropriate behavior online, perhaps, but an online conversation between PR professors[10] asked the question "when does teaching stop?" in response to an offensive comment posted by a graduate of the author's program that, prior to social media, may never have been "overheard" by a professor. McLuhan mandates no value judgments in his tetrad; the answers to the question of obsolescence are not necessarily meant to reflect negatively on the medium itself. One perspective is that social media blurs the line between public and private. Hannah Arendt calls this dangerous, blurred area "the social." For Arendt, the social threatens the public and private, especially when considering the effects of mass society: "mass society not only destroys the public realm but the private as well, deprives men not only of their place in the world but of their private home, where they once felt sheltered against the world and where, at any rate, even those excluded from the world could find a substitute in the warmth of the hearth and the limited reality of family life."[11] One of the reasons why I don't friend students on Facebook is because I feel I'm invading their space, and they (unknowingly) invade mine. I'd like to consider my students based on their performance in class and in our interpersonal interactions, not based on the amount of drunken photos they may or may not have posted on their Facebook page.

In an interview with John Durham Peters, Claire L. Kane gets at this question of obsolescence, asking Peters what the implications digital communications have for future generations:

> JDP: [...] Harold Innis would note that our current digital documentation has a classic space-bias. How long will these things exist that we constantly archive? I conserve my journal scribblings on my computer—should I print them on archival paper and get the right ink?
>
> CLK: Can't you just burn a DVD?
>
> JDP: You are optimistic. We can still read papyrus more than 2,000 years later. Its decoding technology is expensive—literacy and knowledge of the language—but relatively immune to technical failure although not to civilizational collapse. I am skeptical whether in 2,000 years we will be able to read DVDs. Or 50 years. Or 25. Think of vinyl records. I threw a big pile of floppy disks away a few years ago. They held years' worth of work. I figured—ha ha—I could make life easier for some future historian.
>
> CLK: You could upgrade to new technology once DVDs become obsolete.
>
> JDP: Then we have a game of chains of custody, where you need to be constantly updating. But Papyrus is time-bound from the get-go. You only need to make sure the rats and robbers don't get to it. If it's kept in a dry place in Qumran, the place where the Dead Sea Scrolls were discovered, it's safe.[12]

Peters' comment about vinyl records segues into McLuhan's third question, concerning the multiple positions a tool, media, or artifact can hold in a society: "What recurrence or retrieval of earlier actions and services is brought into play simultaneously by the new form? What older, previously obsolesced ground is brought back and inheres in the new form?"[13] Although Peters is correct about the floppy discs (no one is touting a "3.5-inch floppy revival"), the "resurgence" of vinyl records is one possible example of the recurrence or earlier actions driven by the new media. Sales of music began to decline because of music filesharing, an early form of social media, reaching new heights in 2001 with Napster and broadband Internet: "Online music sharing had abruptly gone from being a tech-geek hobby to a mainstream activity."[14] Apple revitalized the music industry (and Apple itself) with an emphasis on individuality and portability in June 2002 with the release of a Windows-compatible iPod and the iTunes store. Consumers could purchase one song from one album and store it on the iPod with hundreds of other songs. Recently, the trend toward digital music finds itself coming back around to analog, specifically vinyl records, because of perceived sound quality. Proponents of vinyl say a compressed digital audio file is inferior in quality and experience to vinyl,[15] while researchers hypothesize that the quality is in the ear of the hearer: "Consistent with earlier research in audio quality, even experienced and well practiced listeners seem to prefer whatever quality they are used to hearing rather than sound of the highest quality and fidelity."[16] Despite this debate, in 2010 sales of vinyl increased 14 percent over 2009, which is a new record for vinyl since 1991[17] with indie and classic rock comprising most of the sales. Whether driven by nostalgia, perceived quality, or increased coolness quotient, the resurgence of vinyl illustrates the "previously obsolesced ground . . . brought back and inheres in the new form" that McLuhan describes. Music file sharing was an early form of social media; unfortunately, it turned out to be illegal. Digitizing music eventually led to the revitalization of Apple through the iPod,[18] which emphasized individuality and portability. Consumers could purchase one song from one album and store it on the iPod with hundreds of other songs. If listeners really can't distinguish between a digital file and an analog recording, then what might be driving the resurgence of vinyl records is the desire for authenticity, which will be examined further in chapter 5.

Another example of the retrieval and inherence of new form is the phenomenon of geolocation in social media. Geolocation allows users to note their geographic location via satellite, IP address, or some other form of geolocation technology. Mozilla Firefox, the Internet browser, offers geolocation services to its users, calling it "location-aware browsing":

> When you visit a location-aware website, Firefox will ask you if you want to share your location. If you consent, Firefox gathers information about nearby wireless access points and your computer's IP address. Then Firefox sends this information to the default geolocation service provider, Google Location Services, to get an estimate of your location. That location estimate is then shared with the requesting website. If you say that you do not consent, Firefox will not do anything.[19]

Other examples include services such as Yelp and Foursquare, which allow users to "check in" at locations and businesses, where you can collect virtual badges or write reviews of the establishments. Adam Rosenberg of the Center for Democracy and Technology states: "As a greater number of location-based features have been rolled out, so, too, has greater attention been given to the potential privacy ramifications brought on by these new trends in social media. Sites like PleaseRobMe and CheckinMania—two sites that aggregate public location status updates from a number of social networks—have given us just a glimpse of how much data is floating out there as we walk the line between "oversharing" and simply "being social."[20] The owners and creators of the PleaseRobMe explain their rationale behind the site: "The danger is publicly telling people where you are. This is because it leaves one place you're definitely not . . . home. So here we are; on one end we're leaving lights on when we're going on a holiday, and on the other we're telling everybody on the Internet we're not home."[21]

How is this an example of McLuhan's third law of media? One is in the tension Rosenberg refers to between privacy and being social. Homeowners pay for insurance against break-ins and theft, purchase home security systems, and take other precautions to protect their home from being burglarized. Home security systems depend on the ability of a central monitoring system that knows the status of your house—your *location*—at all times. At the same time, geolocation services increase the risk to homes that insurance and alarm systems attempt to reduce in the first place. Technology that was potentially isolating, serving as a fortress protecting a home, has been brought back into play as social connector, if only superficially.

The final question of McLuhan's tetrad is "When pushed to the limits of its potential (another complementary action), the new form will tend to reverse what had been its original characteristics. What is the reversal potential of the new form?" In this case, Ong's notion of secondary orality might help with the response to this question.[22] Oren Soffer describes the four eras of orality prior to this moment and then adds his own fifth era:

> The first was 'primary orality,' in which no writing technology existed; the second was the 'residual-manuscript orality' of the Middle Ages, in which writing was strongly influenced by the hegemonic oral culture; the third was the highly literate era of 'print culture,' in which the influence of orality decreased dramatically; and the fourth era is 'secondary orality,' in which texts are written or read on radio and television 'Digital orality' constitutes the fifth, relatively new and diachronically last, era, in which orality is entirely written.[23]

Soffer's idea of a fifth, digital orality is an exploration of the phenomenon of computer-mediated communication (CMC) and short messages service (SMS), also known as texting, where instead of speaking, we are recording our thoughts that we would normally articulate orally into an online environment. Soffer argues that CMC and SMS constitute a new orality, past Ong's secondary orality, because these forms resemble the spoken word much more so than the text written for the television or radio that Ong describes in secondary orality. Unlike e-mail, which is relatively static and asynchronous, online chatting and texting necessitate immediate response to continue the conversation: "in a synchronic forum, the reaction time is crucial any delay in response can be disruptive,[24] indicating a technical lag or a problem of attitude of the sender. When the chat involves several people, delays can interrupt the linearity and progress of the conversation and undermine the sequence of turns."[25]

In addition, communication style adapts to the medium not just because of technology but also because of the nature of the space in which the communication is occurring. Being a "chat room," the virtual space is already closer to oral communication than written communication the metaphor of chatting in a room reflects the social and physically present nature of the communication.[26] The abbreviations that rely on the sound of a letter imitating a word (like b4) and virtual utterances that attempt to convey nonverbal communication and tone (for example, "um, yeah" is a sarcastic response) found in CMC and SMS language demonstrate the blend of orality and literacy because of what Soffer describes, "The rigidity of linguistic patterns is liquidized through the creative use of individual agents, who create and recreate a new expressive style to match their social targets."[27]

What about this type of communication has the potential to reverse to its old characteristics, as McLuhan posits? Soffer explains that not only is digital orality different than secondary orality in its spoken and uttered characteristics but it actually goes back to silence, which is a characteristic of the third area of print culture. Texting and chatting online are generally done in silence. The potential for reversal in this medium is that it moves back to print culture and that it rejects the mass communication characteristics of Ong's secondary orality, which orally transmits prepared texts to what is usually noted as "McLuhan's 'global village.'"[28]

McLuhan's four laws of media, when applied to social media, provide us fruitful avenues for inquiry, and illustrate the breadth of technologies that can be considered "social media." Music file sharing, CMC and SMS, digital archiving, geolocation, and of course, Twitter and Facebook, exhibit the characteristics of social media in that they are user-driven, invite group coordination, connect individuals and organizations, allow non-professionals to engage in content creation, and permit comment on public content. One avenue for inquiry is Ong's understanding of secondary orality and the history of oral versus literate culture, which may provide more depth to the discussion of social media as a "breakthrough" technology in this historical moment.

Orality and Literacy: The Ancient Debate

Soffer explains that concerns about social media as a new form of communication have occurred since ancient times: "The emergence of CMC was accompanied by fears about its social influences, in particular, concern about the impact of Internet use on social relationships. Of course, apocalyptic prophesies about the social impact of new communication technologies are nothing new. In the same spirit, Plato warned that writing would erode memory and that written texts could fall in the hands of those who would misunderstand or even defile them.[29] The Church perceived print to be Satan's invention.[30] Before jumping to the conclusion that social media technologies are game-changers and that we've never seen this type of technology before, we should seek a historical frame of reference for dealing with the implications of social media on human communication. Walter Ong[31] explains that the novelty of social media is really not novel: "Most persons are surprised, and many distressed, to learn that essentially the same objections commonly urged today against computers were urged by Plato in the *Phaedrus*[32] and in the *Seventh Letter* against writing."[33] For a helpful perspective on these concerns (both founded and unfounded) about communication technology shifts, we can remember the story of Theuth and Thamus from these two Platonic works.

Plato's Socrates describes the problems with writing using the myth of Theuth as the vehicle for the argument. First Theuth, the Egyptian god of writing, proudly describes his invention to Thamus, the king of the gods, who in response tells Theuth that writing is not the wonderful invention he thinks it is. Thamus describes the negative effects writing will have on memory, because no one will learn anything when they can just refer to the written word, and he also tells Theuth that writing will allow people to have the illusion of wisdom without actually being wise.[34] Socrates then warns Phaedrus that, similar to paintings, writing only seems to be "living" but they cannot actually respond in any way other than repeating what is written, and finally, that bad ideas written down cannot defend themselves, especially since they can be read by anyone, not just the intended audience:

> Besides, once a thing is committed to writing it circulates equally among those who understand the subject and those who have no business with it; a writing cannot distinguish between suitable and unsuitable readers. And if it is ill-treated or unfairly abused it always needs its parent to come to its rescue; it is quite incapable of defending or helping itself.[35]

For Plato, writing will cause a deterioration of memory because facts that had to be remembered can now be written down and referred to as often as necessary. Although Ong describes the contemporary response as parents who are concerned that because their children may use calculators, their math skills will decline, an even more recent discussion is that search engines have the same distressing effect on memory. Why retain facts when you can Google them? The irony is that we depend on other humans for information as much as we do computers. In a study that examined the effects of Google searching on memory, Sparrow et al. concluded "It may be no more than nostalgia at this point, however, to wish we were less dependent on our gadgets. We have become dependent on them to the same degree we are dependent on all the knowledge we gain from our friends and co-workers and lose if they are out of touch. The experience of losing our Internet connection becomes more and more like losing a friend."[36] Ong compares Plato's list of writing's faults to the advent of computers, such as the idea that one cannot interrogate the written word because the response will only be a repetition of the same words: "if you ask a text, you get back nothing except the same, often stupid, words which called for your question in the first place. In the modern critique of the computer, the same objection is put, 'Garbage in, garbage out.'"[37] Plato's critique of writing's unintended audiences people who can't or shouldn't be reading the text echoes in the current historical moment of social media. Clay Shirky explains that we understand the difference between our loved one saying "I love you" and hearing a character on TV say "I love you." Social media, however, confuses a one-to-one communication with one-to-many.[38] Chapter 4 explores this tension between audience and social media in further detail.

We know Plato's position on writing because he relied on writing to make his arguments. Ong calls this "technologizing the word"—and after this happens, there's no going back: "Once the word is technologized, there is no effective way to criticize what technology has done with it without the aid of the highest technology available. Moreover, the new technology is not merely used to convey the critique; in fact, it brought the critique into existence."[39] An example of Ong's argument is the December 2011 redesign of Facebook's user profile page, called "Timeline." After the significant redesign, which included a cover photo that is always public, many Facebook users complained on Facebook. Using tools such as groups, tagging others in status updates, and sharing links to articles criticizing the redesign, Facebook users offered their negative responses to the redesign using Facebook, illustrating Ong's assertion that the new technology doesn't just carry the critique, it allows the critique to exist. On AllFacebook, "an unofficial Facebook blog," Jackie Cohen observes "The same people who squawk the loudest about resisting timeline will be the ones who ultimately take up the most space in your news feed with updates on curation of their new advanced profiles."[40] Despite the outcry, Facebook's appearance remained redesigned and the rollout continued.

Reifying Communication

Ong explains that one of the benefits of writing is that it *is* artificial. Orality is natural to humanity, while writing is a tool that enables us to be better humans: "To say writing is artificial is not to condemn it but to praise it. Like other artificial creations and indeed more than any other, it is utterly invaluable and indeed essential for the realization of fuller, interior, human potentials."[41] Writing enables the tool of social media, which, in the same way, offers fruitful avenues for human development. Ong is not saying that all writing is good; instead, he is showing us that writing can lead to an enlightened form of humanity as much as it can lead to evil and debasement. Neil Postman, on the other hand, is more skeptical about the role of the tool in a formerly tool-less effort, offering the story of French physician René-Théophile-Hyacinthe Laënnec's invention of the stethoscope in 1816 as a cautionary tale. Laënnec's invention allowed physicians to learn more about their patients from their physical symptoms than their spoken accounts: "interposing an instrument between patient and doctor would transform the practice of medicine...Doctors would lose their ability to conduct skillful examinations and rely more on machinery than on their own experience and insight."[42] Postman warns that overemphasis on the tools (technology) removes human agency and results in reification, which is "converting an abstract idea (mostly, a word) into a thing."[43] Reification is especially harmful when applied to ideas like intelligence and beauty; according to Postman, "We use the word 'intelligence' to refer to a variety of human capabilities of which we approve. There is no such thing as 'intelligence.' It is a word, not a thing, and a word of a very high order of abstraction. But if we believe it to be a thing like the pancreas or liver, then we will believe scientific procedures can locate it and measure it."[44]

In the study of social media, especially of its use in organizations, reification abounds. The act of communicating using social media is reified: popular and trade press articles offer "how-to" be on Facebook, Twitter, LinkedIn, and other technologies as if the technology was the end in itself. Online, an organization is reified to the extent that decision makers in an organization decide to use social media and then forget that an actual human needs to do the communicating. In integrated marketing communication, the brand is intangible but it is reified so that "protecting the brand" becomes a mantra, as if we can put the brand in a fireproof safe. Reification requires a standard measurement instrument; how can we objectively measure "brand loyalty"? How can we calculate the ROI of Twitter? How can we monetize a YouTube video featuring a singing dog? A specific example of this type of reification can be seen in the public relations industry's heated ongoing debates about the idea of a standardized set of measures. Some PR practitioners and most scholars reject AVEs (advertising value equivalents) in favor of a more specific, PR-related measure, and PR industry opinion leaders from around the world have responded with the Barcelona Principles, which outline approaches to measuring PR outcomes that go beyond calculating media placement. One of the principles states, "Social media can and should be measured."[45] However, as Grupp notes, the movement toward measurement relies on a heavily quantitative platform: "Some researchers[46] suggest that in addition to being descriptive, PR research is dominated by a short-term quantitative tradition."

The reification of a measurement instrument can obfuscate the human nature of communication, supplanting people with objective data. Evidence, which provides support for decisions and discourages emotivism, does not always require an instrument. An overemphasis on the instrument as opposed to the evidence can also mislead practitioners into thinking that better tools bring more control, resulting in absolutes that are neither realistic nor attainable. Reification ignores what Aristotle called "the golden mean" the space between excess and deficiency.[47] Reification makes communication a technique, and Ronald C. Arnett and Pat Arneson explain the danger of technique based on Martin Buber's understanding of dialogue:

> Buber's dialogue rebuffs answers that appear too neat and clean, but are actually abstract and miss genuine connections to a given situated moment . . . Buber did not introduce techniques that could be universally applied across various situations; instead, he pointed to concepts that must be applied differently in each historical moment.[48]

The humanistic tradition reminds us that public relations is an ongoing conversation between and among people, not an instrument, like Laënnec's stethoscope, to be used on subjects that can easily be measured. This is not to say that measurement in public relations is bad or evil; on the contrary, it makes public relations less emotivistic[49] and more rhetorical to base claims on evidence rather than personal preference. However, the emphasis on investing time and resources in finding an appropriate instrument elevates this aspect of public relations evaluation and removes it from a context of ethics, education, and theory-grounded public relations.

Chirographic Culture

Ong describes the effects of a chirographic culture on our communication: "Willingness to live with the 'media' model of communication shows chirographic conditioning."[50] This means that when we describe media, we are actually describing how communication reaches us through the instruments of media as opposed to the act of communicating, which is uniquely human and cannot be replicated by machine. When he refers to "chirographic conditioning" he is referring to the shift from oral culture to chirographic (writing) culture that has impacted human communication and human organization how people relate and communicate. Ong's seminal work, *Orality and Literacy*, outlines this shift and the implications it has had on human history and existence. The move from orality to literacy from an oral to a chirographic culture changed the way we communicate. Since communication is a human pursuit, then it follows that changing communication changes us. With the shift to a chirographic culture, the implications of social media as a text become more pronounced.

Social Media: Ephemeral and Permanent Texts

The ephemerality of social media belies its permanence. Fleeting moments of communication become infinitely fixed on someone's hard drive or in someone's mind. *The Social Network*[51] illustrates this tension. The film's first scene shows Mark Zuckerberg's girlfriend, Erica, breaking up with him. As the movie tells it, he is so destroyed by the break-up that it drives him to eventually create Facebook. The evening he gets dumped, he returns to his room, gets drunk, and writes a blog post excoriating his ex-girlfriend, her family, and all the women of Boston University. When he sees her again, a few months later, he tries to apologize, but Erica responds, "The internet is not written in pencil, Mark, it's written in ink. And you published that Erica Albright's a bitch right before you made some ignorant crack about my family's name, my bra size and then rated women based on their hotness."[52] The metaphor of pencil versus pen, referring to the indelibility of content published on the Internet, reverberates in the dialogue-rich movie that examines one of the most significant social media sites, Facebook. However, Michael Leff reminds us that Aaron Sorkin was not the first to consider the pencil/pen metaphor: "One of Jacques Derrida's best known principles is that erasures always leave their traces."[53]

One of the traces of these erasures is the Wayback Machine[54], a product of the online library, Internet Archive. In partnership with the Smithsonian Institute, the site archives web sites—including audio and video files—from 1996 forward, cataloging and organizing this mountain of data as a virtual library. The site explains, "Libraries exist to preserve society's cultural artifacts and to provide access to them. If libraries are to continue to foster education and scholarship in this era of digital technology, it's essential for them to extend those functions into the digital world. Many early movies were recycled to recover the silver in the film. The Library of Alexandria—an ancient center of learning containing a copy of every book in the world—was eventually burned to the ground. Even now, at the turn of the twenty-first century, no comprehensive archives of television or radio programs exist."[55]

The Wayback Machine is not the only effort to preserve "born-digital" materials. Usenet, described in the first section of this chapter, first went live in 1979. This text-based service that originated between Duke and UNC-Chapel Hill offered the growing tech culture a way to communicate and share files.[56] Usenet is still used, but Google has archived twenty years' of Usenet articles into its Google Groups service over 800 million messages from 1981 forward.[57] Not only does Google house the archive but they have curated specific articles (discussions) and threads in a timeline format, such as "Tim Berners-Lee's announcement of what became the World Wide Web or Linus Torvalds' [the creator of Linux] post about his 'pet project.'"[58]

The amount of content being archived moves the fleeting communication of the tweet, the post, the comment, or the tag into a fixed state. The creators of the Wayback Machine, the Internet Archive, describe this as moving the ephemeral to the artifact: "Internet libraries can change the content of the Internet from ephemera to enduring artifacts of our political and cultural lives."[59] It is still difficult to comprehend the lasting presence of a tweet that says "I had steak for dinner" but the reality is that these voluminous data remains as a trace for much longer than most users even those who were at Duke and UNC-Chapel Hill in 1979 originally expected.

In addition to the volume of content, the "ownership" of content and who may or may not "erase" it from its online state is always in question. Pinterest, a social networking site that mimics a bulletin board where users can "pin" images to their virtual boards, recognized the challenge to ownership of content when it revised its Terms of Service, Acceptable Use Policy, and Privacy Policy, effective April 6, 2012. Pinterest launched in early 2010 and as of December 2011 had over 7 million unique users, many of whom were clicking on the pinned image and following through to a personal or business site.[60] One major caveat to users that most didn't realize was that Pinterest was granted rights to sell all content posted. If I posted a photo of a dessert I made or a particularly cute photo of my dog, Pinterest could sell it, since I'd granted the service these rights when I signed up for an account. These same terms applied to any businesses posting content. Because of its visual appeal and heavy female user demographic, many fashion and home décor brands used Pinterest as a portal to their sites. So I could repin a copyrighted photo from *Better Homes and Gardens*[61] to my own Pinterest board, and Pinterest could claim the same rights to that photo as it could to my personal photo of my latest culinary masterpiece. Pinterest announced on their own blog on March 23, 2012, that they would be changing their terms and policies, explaining,

> When we first launched Pinterest, we used a standard set of terms. We think that the updated Terms of Service, Acceptable Use Policy, and Privacy Policy are easier to understand and better reflect the direction our company is headed in the future…Our original Terms stated that by posting content to Pinterest you grant Pinterest the right for us to sell your content. Selling content was never our intention and we removed this from our updated Terms.[62]

Whether selling content was ever their intention (a dubious claim, since one of the biggest challenges for sustaining a social networking site is monetization) Pinterest recognized the free-for-all its service had become and attempted to self-regulate by establishing some guidelines for who owned what on its site. Pinterest also edited their Acceptable Use Policy to address types of content that are regulated.

An even more complex understanding of the trace left behind after erasure is in the case of Harvard University and UCLA sociologists who created a dataset of a cohort of freshmen college students culled from Facebook data. In their press release, they state "With permission from Facebook and the university in question, we first accessed Facebook on March 10 and 11, 2006 and downloaded the profile and network data provided by one cohort of college students."[63] The researchers assured the public and the university's IRB that the identifying information of the subjects was either deleted or encoded after the profiles were downloaded. However, based on the researchers' press release, which described the data as students at "a diverse private college in the Northeast U.S. . . . of the 1640 freshmen students enrolled at the college, 97.4% maintained Facebook profiles at the time of download and 59.2% had last updated their profiles within 5 days."[64] The researchers then collected the data three more times in the spring semesters ending in 2009. The university also allowed the researchers to access housing records for the class which made these data even more valuable. Because the National Science Foundation partially funded the project, the Facebook dataset had to be released to the public after an application process. However, the codebook for the data, which included demographic and psychographic descriptions and frequencies (including race, ethnicity, major, and home state or country), was available online without an application. According to Zimmer, the professor at UW-Milwaukee who matched the details from the press release with the information from the codebook, the press release, and other public comments, "the source of the data was quickly narrowed down from over 2000 possible colleges and universities to a list of only seven.[65] The enrollment numbers, geographic location, and private status of the college easily culled the list, which included Harvard College. Zimmer then compared the codebook's list of majors to those at the seven institutions; only Harvard College "offered the specific variety of the subjects' majors that are listed in the codebook, such as Near Eastern Languages and Civilizations, Studies of Women, Gender, and Sexuality, and Organismic and Evolutionary Biology."[66] Combined with a statement from the researchers regarding students' housing arrangements (which is specific to Harvard as well), Zimmer deduced the plausible identification of the dataset as being the Harvard College class of 2010.

Several factors make this story a nexus of research ethics, privacy issues, IRB oversight, and unauthorized use of data. The most pertinent to the idea that content on the Internet is a trace from an erasure per Derrida is that the "consent" by Facebook was manual, meaning research assistants (other Harvard graduate and undergraduate students) downloaded the Facebook profiles that were open to *them*. Of the 1,446 students on Facebook (out of the total 1,640), only 152 had a profile that existed but that an RA couldn't see and only 42 were not viewable at all. This means that students who made their profile available to everyone in the Harvard network but not to the public were actually granting access to the researchers on the project who normally wouldn't be able to view the profiles. Because the RAs were in the Harvard network, they had access to these profiles that the researchers (and everyone else outside of Harvard's network) did not. In the meantime, the students updated their profiles believing that they could delete photos or posts, when any deleted information was actually remaining in the archive of data that the researchers collected, leaving an unknown trace after its erasure.

A Rhetorical Approach to Social Media

This incident captures the paradoxical nature of social media: traces of content remain long after those who created the content move on, mature, or in this example, graduate. The virtual residue of our existence is left behind, freezing a trace of our humanity for posterity. We are present in the creation of this communication, yet we are distanced by its mediated nature and our inability to "see" with whom we are communicating. One way we can understand this "presence" is to situate it in epideictic rhetoric, the mode of rhetoric dealing with the present. According to Aristotle, epideictic rhetoric "is, properly speaking, concerned with the present, since all men praise and blame in view of the state of things existing at the time, though they often find it useful to recall the past and to make guesses at the future."[67]

The classic form of epideictic rhetoric is the funeral oration, which praises the deceased and holds his or her virtuous actions (mainly his in Ancient Greece) up as an example for the living to follow; it reinforces the shared civic virtue agreed upon by a society.[68] In an extension to this understanding of epideictic, Rosenfield interprets Aristotle through an etymological frame: "the term epideictic comes from *epideixis* ('to shine or show forth') . . . More precisely the word suggests an exhibiting or making apparent (in the sense of showing or highlighting) what might otherwise remain unnoticed or invisible . . . . Epideictic, therefore, acts to unshroud men's notable deeds in order to let us gaze at the aura glowing from within."[69] Rollins argues that Rosenfield releases epideictic rhetoric from its emphasis on display, ornamentation, and the ceremonial because "its audience is *not* required to impose judgment on the matters that appear in the epideictic speech." Rosenfield also interprets Aristotle's assertion that epideictic rhetoric focuses on matters of praise and blame as problematic:

> I believe that epideictic served a more significant theoretical role than a wastebasket for classifying lesser orations in the rhetorical domain. I contend, in brief, that we misconstrue epideictic when we hold its fundamental tactics to ben praise and blame. What is involved instead maybe more accurately thought of as "acknowledgement" and "disparagement," the recognition of what *is*, (goodness, grace, intrinsic excellence) or the refusal to so recognize in a moment of social inspiration. In either case the experience afforded the participant is the opportunity of beholding reality impartially as witnesses of Being.[70]

Rosenfield takes this last idea of audience as bearing witness to be markedly different than the role of critic or assessor, which is necessary in judicial rhetoric (i.e., serving as a juror) or deliberative (i.e., serving as a voter). Epideictic rhetoric that bears witness and acknowledges what *is* is as vital for a functioning society as rhetoric that delivers justice or decides upon a future course of action. For this reason, Rosenfield suggests that epideictic oratory 'calls upon us to join with our community in giving thought to what we witness."[71] In social media, whether composed of millions or dozens, the community bears witness to the words and images emerging every second. Rollins explains the limitations of Rosenfield's work as being tied to the universal; namely, he does not put the theory into action to "consider epideictic rhetoric as a singular response to its defining occasion," so Rollins refers to Derrida.

According to Rollins, "Derrida is one of our most accomplished and sensitive epideictic orators," in part because he delivered so many funeral eulogies for his friends such as Barthes, Foucault, Deleuze, Levinas, and Blanchot. The situation of the funeral oration where people gather in each other's presence to grieve the dead who is no longer present offers a "paradoxical notion of the simultaneously present and distant friend."[72] Social media is similar in this paradox; in fact, it is eerie in its resemblance to Derrida's characterization of mourning as "hanging on to images and memories that keep friends with us . . . what Derrida's funeral speeches do, however, is allow us to respond to our dead friends, now figured as collections of images that we can visualize and mobilize, while still leaving them to their infinite otherness."[73]

This may seem like an odd marriage of funeral oratory and social media, but it reminds us that we cannot take the communication that occurs online in these channels lightly. We are privy to intimate moments yet absent in physical presence. The trivial matters of social media the recording of likes, dislikes, shares, posts, tweets in fact, *matter*. They are part of, as Arnett and Arneson call it, "the mud of everyday life . . ." and reflect a potential for dialogue, which is "invited as we address limits, flaws, and difficulties presented by the nitty-gritty reality of common life together in a situated historical moment."[74] In chapter 3, I examine the nature of social media as epideictic rhetoric and, as such, how a rhetorical understanding of social media offers a hermeneutic entrance into what social media as human communication in the context of the marketplace can realize.

Why Humanities?

An overreliance on the social scientific roots of the communication discipline in fields such as integrated marketing communication, public relations, and advertising lead practitioners and academics to ignore the humanist, interpretive, rhetorical approach which views these applied fields as examples of human beings in dialogue, and even subordinates qualitative research because of its lack of hard data (anything qualitative, like positive or negative media hits, is still quantified in this tradition). While quantitative and social scientific research are necessary tools that help us understand communication, the humanistic approach invites a perspective that situates lived practices in the historical moment while being attentive to a tradition born two millennia ago.

This book hopes to characterize the social media phenomenon as neither of all-consuming importance nor of inconsequential trivialization. It is a form of human communication, and as such should be considered with the same care and attention that human communication warrants. Integrated marketing communication (IMC) faces similar critiques; chapter 2 examines these critiques in more depth.

Notes

1. Cara Bonnett, "A Piece of Internet History," *Duke Today* 2010, http://today.duke.edu/2010/05/usenet.html (accessed March 6, 2013).

2. Jeff Bercovici, "Who Coined 'Social Media'? Web Pioneers Compete for Credit," *Forbes* 2010, www.forbes.com/sites/jeffbercovici/2010/12/09/who-coined-social-media-web-pioneers-compete-for-credit/ (accessed March 6, 2013).

3. Charlene Li and Josh Bernoff, *Groundswell: Winning in a World Transformed by Social Technologies* (Boston: Harvard Business Press, 2008), 11.

4. Clay Shirky, *Here Comes Everybody: The Power of Organizing Without Organizations* (London: Penguin Books, 2009), 20.

5. Lance Strate, "A Media Ecology Review," *Communication Research Trends* 23 (2004): 7.

6. Strate, "A Media Ecology Review," 7.

7. Marshall McLuhan and Eric McLuhan, *Laws of Media: The New Science* (Toronto: University of Toronto Press, 1988), 98.

8. McLuhan and McLuhan, *Laws of Media*, 98.

9. McLuhan and McLuhan, *Laws of Media*, 98.

10. Karen M. Russell, "When does teaching stop?," *Teaching PR* 2011, www.teachingpr.org/teaching_pr/2011/09/when-does-teaching-stop.html (accessed March 6, 2013).

11. Hannah Arendt, *The Human Condition* (Chicago: University of Chicago Press, 1998), 59.

12. Carolyn L. Kane and John D. Peters, "Speaking into the iPhone: An Interview with John Durham Peters, or, Ghostly Cessation for the Digital Age," *Journal of Communication Inquiry* (2010): 131.

13. McLuhan and McLuhan, *Laws of Media*, 98.

14. Kane and Peters, "Speaking into the iPhone," 131.

15. Lucas Mearian, "Forget digital tunes; analog music on the upswing," *Computerworld* 2010, www.computerworld.com/s/article/9187001/Forget_digital_tunes_analog_music_on_the_upswing (accessed March 6, 2013).

16. John Geringer and Patrick Dunnigan, "Listener Preferences and Perception of Digital versus Analog Live Concert Recording," *University of Illinois Press*, no. 145 (2000): 1-13.

17. Matthew Perpetua, "Vinyl Sales Increase Despite Industry Slump," *RollingStone* 2011, www.rollingstone.com/music/news/vinyl-sales-increase-despite-industry-slump-20110106 (accessed March 6, 2013).

18. Jon Chase, "The iPod Turns 10," *Entertainment Weekly* 2011, www.ew.com/ew/article/0,,20538827,00.html (accessed March 6, 2013).

19. "Location-Aware Browsing," *Firefox*, www.mozilla.org/en-US/firefox/geolocation/ (accessed October 23, 2011).

20. Jennifer Leggio, "Toeing the line between privacy and social media," *ZDNet* 2010, www.zdnet.com/blog/feeds/toeing-the-line-between-privacy-and-social-media/2663?tag=content;siu-container (accessed October 23, 2011).

21. "Raising awareness about over-sharing," *Please Rob Me* 2010, http://pleaserobme.com/why (accessed October 23, 2011).

22. Walter J. Ong, *Orality and Literacy* (New York: Routledge, 1982), 132.

23. Oren Soffer, "'Silent Orality': Toward a Conceptualization of the Digital Oral Features in CMC and SMS Texts," *Communication Theory* 20 (2010): 388.

24. Walther J. Pena and J.T. Hancock, "Effects of geographic distribution on dominance perceptions in computer-mediated groups," *Communication Research* 34 (2007): 330.

25. David Crystal, *Language and the Internet* (New York: Cambridge University Press, 2006), 392.

26. Soffer, "Silent Orality," 388.

27. McLuhan and McLuhan, *Laws of Media*, 99.

28. Soffer, "Silent Orality," 390.

29. Drew A. Hyland, "Why Plato Wrote Dialogues," *Philosophy and Rhetoric* 1, no. 1(1968): 39.

30. Soffer, "Silent Orality," 391.

31. Ong, *Orality and Literacy,* 77-78.

32. Stephen Scully, *Plato's Phaedrus* (Newburyport, MA: Focus Publishing, 2003): 274-77.

33. Ludwig Edelstein, *Plato's Seventh Letter* (E.J. Brill: Leiden, Netherlands, 1966): 78.

34. Scully, *Plato's Phaedrus,* 274-75.

35. Scully, *Plato's Phaedrus,* 274-77.

36. Betsy Sparrow, Jenny Liu, and Daniel M. Wegner. "Google Effects on Memory: Cognitive Consequences of Having Information at Our Fingertips," *Science* 333 (2011): 777-778.

37. Ong, *Orality and Literacy,* 78.

38. Shirky, *Here Comes Everybody,* 87.

39. Ong, *Orality and Literacy,* 79.

40. Jackie Cohen, "Tensions Rise Over Facebook Timeline," *AllFacebook* 2012, http://allfacebook.com/facebook-timeline-mandatory_b75224 (accessed August 7, 2011).

41. Ong, *Orality and Literacy,* 80.

42. Neil Postman, *Technopoly: The Surrender of Culture to Technology* (New York: Vintage Books, 1993), 130.

43. Postman, *Technopoly,* 130.

44. Postman, *Technopoly,* 130.

45. Robert W. Grupp, "The Barcelona Declaration of Research Principles," *Institute for Public Relations* 2010, www.instituteforpr.org/2010/06/the-barcelona-declaration-of-research-principles/.

46. Grupp, "The Barcelona Declaration of Research Principles."

47. Aristotle, *Nichomachean Ethics*, Trans. David Ross (Oxford: Oxford University Press, 1998), 1104a16.

48. Ronald C. Arnett and Pat Arneson, *Dialogic Civility in a Cynical Age* (Albany: SUNY Press, 1999), 138.

49. Alasdair MacIntyre, *After Virtue* (Notre Dame: University of Notre Dame, 1999), 173.

50. Ong, *Orality and Literacy,* 173.

51. Aaron Sorkin, *The Social Network,* directed by David Fincher (2010, Los Angeles, Sony Pictures), DVD.

52. Sorkin, *The Social Network.*

53. Michael Leff, "The Habitation of Rhetoric," in *Contemporary Rhetorical Theory: a Reader,* eds. John Louis Lucaites, Celeste Michelle Condit, and Sally Caudill (New York: The Guilford Press, 1987): 54.

54. Butch Lazorchak, "Using Wayback Machine for Research," *The Signal Digital Preservation* 2012, http://blogs.loc.gov/digitalpreservation/2012/10/10950 (accessed October 23, 2011). The name "Wayback Machine" pays homage to The Rocky & Bullwinkle Show and Mr. Peabody's WABAC Machine.

55. "About the Internet Archive," *Internet Archive* 2001, http://archive.org/about/ (accessed October 23, 2011).

56. Andrew Anderson, "a History," *Usenet* 1996, http://tldp.org/LDP/nag/node256.html (accessed October 23, 2011).

57. "20 Year Usenet Timeline," *Google Groups* 2011, www.google.com/googlegroups/archive_announce_20.html (accessed October 23, 2011).

58. "20 Year Usenet Timeline," *Google Groups* 2011, www.google.com/googlegroups/archive_announce_20.html (accessed October 23, 2011).

59. "About the Internet Archive," *Internet Archive.*

60. Jason Falls, "How Pinterest Is Becoming the Next Big Thing in Social Media for Business," *Entrepreneur* 2012, www.entrepreneur.com/article/222740 (accessed October 23, 2011).

61. "Better Homes and Gardens," *Pinterest*, http://pinterest.com/bhg (accessed March 7, 2013).

62. Courteney Palis, "Pinterest Terms of Service Get Updated," *The Huffington Post* 2012, www.huffingtonpost.com/2012/03/26/pinterest-terms-of-service-update-_n_1379486.html (accessed March 6, 2013).

63. Michael Zimmer, "But the data is already public: on the ethics of research in Facebook," *Ethics Information Technology* 12 (2010): 325.

64. Zimmer, "But the data is already public," 325.

65. Zimmer, "But the data is already public," 325.

66. Zimmer, "But the data is already public," 325.

67. Aristotle, *Nichomachean Ethics,* 1358b.

68. Brooke Rollins, "The Ethics of Epideictic Rhetoric: Addressing the Problem of Presence through Derrida's Funeral Orations," *RSQ: Rhetoric Society Quarterly* 35, no. 1 (2005): 6.

69. Rollins, "The Ethics of Epideictic Rhetoric," 10 and Lawrence W. Rosenfield, "The Practical Celebration of Epideictic," *Rhetoric in Transition: Studies in the Nature and Uses of Rhetoric* (University Park: Pennsylvania State University Press, 1980), 135.

70. Rosenfield, "The Practical Celebration of Epideictic," 134.

71. Rollins, "The Ethics of Epideictic Rhetoric," 10.

72. Rollins, "The Ethics of Epideictic Rhetoric," 11.

73. Rollins, "The Ethics of Epideictic Rhetoric," 15.

74. Arnett and Arneson, *Dialogic Civility in a Cynical Age*, 32.

Chapter 2
A History and Philosophy of Integrated Marketing Communication (IMC)

IMC emerged from Northwestern University's Medill School of Journalism in the late 1980s. The seminal work *Integrated Marketing Communications*, by Don E. Schultz, Stanley I. Tannenbaum, and Robert F. Lauterborn, moved marketing communication from the agent-driven four Ps—product, price, promotion, and placement—to the four Cs (consumer, cost, convenience, and communication) and a focus on the interaction with the consumer as a rational person: "Enter a new age of advertising: respectful, not patronizing; dialogue-seeking, not monologic; responsive, not formula-driven, it speaks to the highest point of common interest, not the lowest common denominator.[1] A definition of IMC developed by Schultz and Philip J. Kitchen connects communication, strategy, and business aims: "IMC is a strategic business process used to plan, develop, execute, and evaluate coordinated, measurable, persuasive brand communication programs over time with consumers, customers, prospects, and other targeted, relevant external and internal audiences."[2]

Traditional Marketing vs. IMC

A significant difference between traditional marketing and IMC is that IMC focuses on customer and prospect behavior, not attitudes: "We believe that behavior more clearly indicates what a person will do in the future than do various intention or attitudinal approaches."[3] Focusing on behavior offers a more reliable metric that can actually be measured; it

31

offers an initial approach to aggregating customers and prospective customers.[4] Robert Lavidge and Gary Steiner developed the hierarchy of effects model in 1961 that begins with advertising and defines four stages of attitude development between the advertising message and consumer behavior.[5] IMC scholars such as Don E. Schultz and Heidi Schultz argue that the hierarchy of effects model is a hypothesis that cannot completely explain consumer behavior: "the greatest challenge to the model is that it is hypothetical and, despite its acceptance, there is practically no scientific evidence that it correctly assesses the way the human mind responds to advertising or marketing communication." [6] IMC emphasizes purchasing behavior and works backward to explain attitudes, inverting the model and reorienting the marketing communication process.[7]

While IMC scholars do not presume that IMC is the best or only way to practice marketing communication, they do decry an understanding of IMC as management fad. Anders Gronstedt claims:

> IMC has been an important step in the direction of integrated communications, but an insufficient one, motivated in large part by communications agencies' appetite for more business. [...] Instead of a skin-deep integration of messages and creative execution, this book defines integrated communications as a process of dialogue, interaction, and learning, with the purpose of adding value and cultivating relationships with key customers and stakeholders.[8]

Gronstedt argues for integrated marketing communications as an integral business strategy—one that is necessary for all areas of the organization to own and engage.

Don E. Schultz and Heidi Schultz offer three shifts that occurred in the mid-1980s that drove the development of integrated marketing communication:

- The development and diffusion of digital technology across the entire spectrum of business operations.
- The increasing emphasis on brands and branding as the major competitive differentiating tool.
- The increasing focus on multinationalization and globalization as marketers spread across the traditional geographic boundaries.[9]

These drivers are tied to a focus on accountability—measuring the value that marketing communication programs brought to the organization.

IMC is not a technique, however; it is more than a formula or a methodology that, when executed, brings about desired results. Philip J. Kitchen and Patrick De Pelsmacker argue that IMC "*has the potential to become a driving force if a company takes the steps that lead to its implementation . . .* IMC can be, in fact, what any organization determines it to be."[10] Kitchen and De Pelsmacker warn that organizations must make a significant shift to take these steps that might lead to its implementation, that marketing and marketing communication must become a priority, and time, money, and effort must be committed in order to reframe an organization's understanding of its marketing and communication efforts.[11]

It is this nebulous view of IMC that opens it to criticism for trying to overreach. Joep P. Cornelissen, a corporate communication scholar, claims that IMC doesn't actually do what it claims to do:

> Reviewing the available empirical evidence on one central thesis of IMC theory—the organization of all communication disciplines into a single, integrated department—I argue that rather being *descriptive* of contemporary marketing communications management, the use of IMC theory should rather be seen as rhetorical and ideological, with the purpose of pragmatically edifying and legitimizing practical changes in marketing communications.[12]

Cornelissen's argument hinges on the idea that IMC theory is nothing new, that the idea of "integration" happens whether or not it's called IMC, and that the use of the term IMC is simply to make a more legitimate claim as a marketing and management approach rather than a truly new organizing framework for the traditional IMC areas of advertising, public relations, promotions, marketing communication, direct marketing, event and experiential marketing, and online marketing. To Cornelissen, the term "integrated marketing communication" is really just a good way for IMC to promote itself as the progressive answer to the problems present in marketing communication.

In another critique, some public relations scholars claim that the theory and practice of public relations is rooted in mass communication and reject the idea that IMC could ever include public relations in its reach. David Guth and Charles Marsh, authors of the textbook *Values-Driven Public Relations*, make this claim early in their first chapter:

> Marketing, the central concept in IMC, focuses on consumers. We respectfully suggest that public relations practitioners engage in relationships that go far beyond consumer communications . . . this debate is

indicative of the broader struggle public relations practitioners have faced since the dawn of the 20th century: to have public relations accepted as a separate and significant profession.[13]

Guth and Marsh's argument focuses on the audience of public relations—the audience of IMC is limited to consumers, whereas the audience for public relations is much broader.

While Guth and Marsh describe the conventional naming of audiences in IMC (consumers) and public relations (publics), the limitations of this perspective are especially pronounced in this historical moment. No longer can we designate some of our audience consumers and some publics. The idea that public relations practitioners are developing relationships with groups beyond consumers, so therefore, IMC doesn't have the reach that public relations does, recalls a positivist approach to both public relations and marketing. Publics, target markets, consumers—the search for common ground for these three groups is a much more productive, ethical, and realistic approach that meets the challenges and the opportunities of this postmodern historical moment.

Postmodernity and IMC

IMC in a pluralistic world rejects the agent-driven modernist view of mass communication that can be found in the hierarchy of effects (advertising-based) model of communication, where communication is one-way and linear, moving from media advertising instigated by the marketer and proceeding along a hierarchy of attitudes, knowledge, preference, and conviction to arrive at purchase behavior.[14] A postmodern understanding of IMC moves from this modernist approach to postmodernity, a historical moment marked by narrative contention and metanarrative decline.[15] According to Ronald C. Arnett, "Postmodernity assumes the pragmatic necessity of encountering clashing rhetorics that represent differing narrative traditions with dialectic giving insight into alterity and dialogue permitting the meeting of difference."[16]

However, attention to the postmodern historical moment is different from "postmodernist marketing." Tony Proctor and Philip J. Kitchen describe the latter when they claim that characteristics of postmodernism can be found throughout marketing communication: "Postmodernism argues that perhaps consumers do not really know what they want, only what they do not want . . . Postmodernist approaches shroud the straight marketing question of 'What can be done to satisfy consumer needs and wants?' with ambiguity."[17] The proliferation of products and services available presents too much choice to consumers and a new task to marketers: "it is persuading people to make up their minds in the first place that is now one of the pre-eminent communication issues."[18]

Another example of "postmodernist marketing" is Philip J. Kitchen's "Communications Leviathan."[19] Thomas Hobbes used the metaphor of the Leviathan to describe the forces exerted on humans: "Men are therefore, at best, complicated automata influenced by internal material perceptions of an external material world (Hobbes, 1651, p. 52)."[20] Kitchen extends this metaphor to marketing communication:

> The volume of marketing communications is increasing rapidly . . . such communications represent what has been termed a leviathan. Such a leviathan repeated *ad nauseum* creates a potential to be a form of pollution. However, proof of such pollution created by a marketing communications leviathan has not been presented in this article. What has been presented is that the leviathan has the potential to be a form of pollution.[21]

The combination of the "Communications Leviathan" and the postmodernist marketing perspective identify two possible outcomes: "Do consumers respond to data overload with confusion, existential despair, and the loss of moral identity? Or do they adapt constructively to the Leviathan and become intelligent, cynical, streetwise, circumspect Postmodern Consumers who are just as savvy as advertisers who are trying to persuade them?"[22] Viewing IMC from a "postmodernist marketing" perspective is not the dialectic of productive tensions over a common center that Ronald C. Arnett describes: "Bonhoeffer's view of an interpersonal communication ethic suggests a 'common center'[23] that ties us to something larger and more significant than the individual self."[24] In "postmodernist marketing," the common center is not an option between existential despair and cynicism. Instead, IMC situated in the postmodern historical moment seeks a common center:

> For business, the common center needs to be commitment to increasing the quality of products responsive to the historical situation in which people live, not campaigns to convince one to use the unhelpful. When one meets a historical need, the advertising comes with an implicit "why" the product is important, permitting one to tell about the improvements in the product.[24]

Understanding IMC from a communication perspective can potentially offer this common center.

IMC: Finding Communicative Ground

Simon Torp describes the field of IMC on an x/y axis; in the upper-right quadrant where "not theory-based (non-academic)" and advocates of IMC meet sits "much of the consultancy literature" and "various contributions to non-theoretical publications."[25] In the lower-right quadrant, academic, theory-based IMC advocates such as Don E. Schultz and Tom Duncan reside. In the bottom-left quadrant, Torp places theory-based opponents and skeptics such as James and Larissa Grunig, Joep Cornelissen, and Lars Thørger Christensen. Christensen, Firat, and Torp offer a more flexible approach to IMC that reflects the human elements of communication and organizations:

> As an alternative to the prescriptive differences that we find most often in the field, we ask the question of how the project of integrating communications can coexist with other significant organizational concerns, preferences and agendas, including the call for differentiation, variety, and flexibility in the organizational setting. Is the project of integrated communications, in other words, sophisticated enough to allow organizations to register, manage and adapt to continuous changes and variations in their surroundings?[26]

Although Christensen, Firat, and Torp are concerned about the gap between the "conventional approaches to integrated communications" and their proposed flexible integration approach because of issues of control, rigidity, hierarchy, and conformity as opposed to adaptation and responsiveness, the authors focus on organizational characteristics and context as rather than communication as a theoretical ground. Organizations that are fluid, responsive, and diverse—and organizations that are rigid, static, and unyielding—do not just appear fully formed in a vacuum. They reflect the humans who make up the organization and the communication that ensues. Therefore, a postmodern understanding of integrated marketing communication combines the uncertainty and contingency of our age and, at its best, attempts to find a response that persuades ethically and effectively, acknowledging that there may be more than one good answer to the questions a client asks. This understanding of IMC fits into the rhetorical tradition, which works in response to contingency, particularity, temporality, and locality, based on available knowledge, to determine a sound course of action.

Gerard A. Hauser outlines a rhetorical approach to IMC through the "discursive processes" of a public, which he defines as "the interdependent members of society who hold different opinions about a mutual problem and who seek to influence its resolution through discourse."[27] Hauser explains that the resolution is not always through a public vote:

> A public's members form a collectivity that may manifest their attention to issues through votes but just as often by exercising their buying power, demonstrations of sympathy or opposition, adornments of colored ribbons, debates in classrooms and on factory floors, speeches on library steps or letters to the editor, correspondence with public officials, and other expressions of stance and judgment. They are not pregiven; publics emerge as those who are actively creating and attending to these *discursive processes* for publicizing opinions, for making them felt by others.[28]

Hauser states that members of a public must have rhetorical competence or "a capacity to participate in rhetorical experiences," which includes interpretation, understanding, and flexibility.[29] In IMC, the rhetorical competence and publics in Hauser's model can be seen as a potential middle ground between the moral confusion and savvy cynicism of the postmodern consumer.[30]

J. Michael Sproule traces the shift in rhetoric's emphasis from participation in the public sphere to management of public opinion, explaining the major differences between rhetoric practiced after the turn of the twentieth century (which he calls "the new managerial rhetoric") and the "old" rhetoric practiced from ancient Greece through the late 1800s: "Notwithstanding surface continuities in the forms of American society and persuasion, the shift during the last four generations from oratorical to managerial forms of social control is evident whether one focuses on source, audience, or message."[31] While Sproule offers multiple examples of this shift, including political and governmental rhetoric, his first example is the commercial shift led by Ivy Lee, one of the first public relations practitioners, who became successful:

> By convincing corporations, first, that they could no longer ignore the general social attitudes of the mass audience, and second, that bribes and threats were futile methods to secure favorable press attention in an era of growing professionalism in the institutions of mass communica-

tion . . . coupled with the rise of national advertising—especially institutional ads that promoted a whole industry—corporate public relations
under the Lee format gave business communication its now familiar
status as institutional persuasion often symbolized by key spokesper-
sons.[32]

Sproule argues the old rhetoric and the new managerial rhetoric provide
parameters within which the public must consider competing images in
order to judge their meaning and significance. Sproule also uses the metaphor of the leviathan to describe the proliferation of messages in this
historical moment: "Social influence in today's managerial mode occurs
not in a true public marketplace where vendors for ideas equally set up
their booths. Rather, the American cultural scene more resembles a su-
permarket of images in which large establishments offer to their customers a limited number of brands promoted by a few social leviathans."[33]
The role of the rhetorical educator, Sproule continues, is to help "political consumers" distinguish between the old and new rhetorics and to
equip them with the tools to analyze these competing images.

Robert L. Heath explains the use of rhetoric in public relations.
Because the IMC framework encompasses advertising, public relations,
and other means of communicating between an organization and its audience, Heath's application to public relations is relevant to IMC as a
whole. Heath claims, "Rhetoric is propositional—the intellectual process
by which humans achieve knowledge, understanding, agreement, and
coordinated actions. The rhetorical perspective assumes that ideas are not
eternally dictated, mandated, or taken for granted"[34] The rhetorical perspective of integrated marketing communication (Heath and Carl H. Botan both refer to strategic communication, of which public relations is a
part) allows competing claims to be deliberated in the public sphere.
Heath argues:

> Rhetorical clash of perspectives gives interested parties the dis-
> course means and the public opportunity to examine and cross-
> examine competing views of fact, value, policy, identification, and
> narrative. Such is the case whether we are examining public policy
> perspectives or considering which product is the best value and
> most likely to satisfy our wants or needs. These are the contexts in
> which public relations operates.[35]

A rhetorical perspective to IMC is not limited to a series of rhetorical
lenses through which we can analyze artifacts or messages. Through
rhetoric, we interpret and share the meaning of messages.

Another area of rhetoric found in strategic communication (which includes public relations and IMC) is Carl H. Botan's application of C.S. Peirce's semiotic theory to the functioning of publics. Botan distinguishes between audiences and publics: "those seeking to address a public often envision a more enduring and complex relationship than do those seeking to address an audience."[36] Much like the consumer-focused orientation in IMC, the semiotic perspective in strategic communication considers not only who constitutes a public but also what actions and communication members of a public engage in to arrive at a conclusion. According to Botan, the semiotic concept of rhetoric

> Conceptualizes pure rhetoric as an endless process by which signs give birth to other signs. This dynamic conception of rhetoric suggests that a sign (representamen) is rhetorically alive when it is able to produce other signs, that is, productive . . . this view . . . suggests that one of a public's (or organization's) most important functions is to keep its representamen productive. Thus, any communicative activity on the part of a public is, *a priori*, rhetorical in the sense that it affects the survival of a representamen.[37]

Viewed semiotically, a public's function is to engage in "an *ongoing process of agreement upon an interpretation.*"[38] Members of a public must find agreement when interpreting signs (i.e., strategic messages) in order to keep the conversation going. F. Byron Nahser refers to C.S. Peirce's work as extended by Josiah Royce to explain the social aspect of interpretation as: "essentially a *social* process, applicable as much to the religious realm as to science. That is, both scientists and religious communities are communities of inquirers who seek truth, and who interpret and reinterpret signs in a shared endeavor."[39]

The theory and practice of branding, a component of IMC, requires interpretation of signs as a shared endeavor. Tony Proctor and Philip J. Kitchen offer four questions that consumers ask when confronted with brands:

- What does the company behind the brands stand for?
- What values does it personify?
- What does it do?
- What personalities are running the company?[40]

This view of IMC claims that consumer behavior can be examined from "a postmodern theoretical perspective which emphasizes knowledge interpretation through metaphor"[41]

Although the rhetoric and philosophy of IMC most often reflects its roots in the humanities, several models of strategic communication relate both to humanities and social sciences. One of these is James E. Grunig's four models of public relations. The four models are press agentry (one-way asymmetrical), public information (one-way symmetrical), two-way asymmetrical, and two-way symmetrical. They fall along a spectrum of direction and intended effect and are "representations of the values, goals, and behaviors held or used by organizations when they practice public relations"[42] The two-way symmetrical model is the social scientific name for a dialogic approach to public relations, while Carl H. Botan classifies the press agentry, public information, and two-way asymmetrical models as technician or monologic approaches. The technician approach is problematic because "it lends itself quite readily to . . . an instrumentalizing process because it focuses only on getting what the client wants. Implicit in this approach is the idea that practitioners should view publics either as a sources of trouble for the client or as the possessor of something the client would like to acquire, such as money or votes."[43] As such, privileging the technician has significant negative ethical implications for the theory and practice of IMC.

Theorizing and practicing public relations and integrated marketing communication (which can be categorized as strategic communication) from a dialogic perspective connects communication ethics and rhetoric, according to Carl H. Botan:

> Consistent with the human nature and dialogic views of ethics (discussed more fully by Johannesen, 1996), the dialogic approach to communication shares with the rhetorical approach the view that humans are uniquely equipped to use symbols and that it is this ability which sets humans apart from other creatures . . . a dialogic view . . . sees communication partners as ends in themselves. From the dialogic perspective practitioners would begin from the assumption that target publics have interpretations of the world that are as varied and valid as the client's interpretations. They would assume that the real goal is not reducing public to the service of the client through instrumental mastery but joining with the publics in the process of negotiating new mutual understanding.[44]

Although one cannot guarantee that every public relations or IMC practitioner will act ethically and rhetorically by engaging in dialogic communication, the potential for what Robert L. Heath calls "the good use of rhetoric" increases with attentiveness to multiple interpretations, the symbol-using capability of humans, and the idea that publics (and organizations) are not means to an end but ends in themselves. Rhetoric's relationship to ethics is especially significant in the realm of integrated marketing communication and its subsets of public relations, advertising, and other forms of promotional communication.

IMC and Communication Ethics

An examination of IMC ethics reflects IMC's joint lineage in the business and communication disciplines. Marketing ethics and communication ethics are two different approaches to problems across the theory and practice of IMC. A review of the marketing ethics literature provides a snapshot of the problems encountered in marketing theory and practice. Sid Lowe et al. articulate the necessity of moving marketing from "amoral science" to "moral art": "The dominance of marketing by *the amoral scientism of the logical empiricists* has led to material enslavement of modern societies."[45] Lowe et al. do not suggest abolishing market economies. Instead, they suggest that "marketing needs to promote a slowing down of frenetic consumption and reduce the speed of global material greed and instant gratification."[46] In order to accomplish this, the authors argue that "we need to be prepared to initiate a discourse related to values and to view the task of marketing as a moral art."[47]

In their study of how people evaluate the ethicality of marketing activities, R. Eric Reidenbach and Donald P. Robin posit that the majority of marketing ethics literature is based on two moral philosophies— deontological and utilitarian. Deontological ethics "focus on moral obligations that should be binding or necessary for proper conduct."[48] Utilitarianism "argues that one should choose the alternative that has the greatest good for the greatest number of people." [49] Reidenbach and Robin add egoism, relativism, and justice to deontological and utilitarian philosophies of ethics for the purposes of their study, but conclude that no one ethical philosophy explains an individual's evaluation of an ethical dilemma.[50] Shelby Hunt and Scott Vitell offer another marketing ethics theoretical model, which combines the deontological and utilitarian ethical approaches.[51] Hunt and Vitell present one of the pitfalls of the utilitarian perspective: "whose good is to be maximized? The good of the individual? Or the good of society in general?" along with the criticism of the deontological philosophy: "deontological theories do not take the promotion of 'the good' seriously enough."[52] Asking the question "what is the 'good' itself?" does not occur in either set of theoretical model. This lack of attention to the good itself limits the use of marketing ethical approaches in IMC. Communication ethics, however, questions how we apprehend the good along with the good itself and provides a more fruitful orientation to integrated marketing communication ethics.

An example of the problem of choosing one "good" above all others is Carl H. Botan's explanation of the problematic ethical orientation of the technician approach to strategic communication and public relations as based on ". . . craft and partisan values. In this view what is labeled *good* public relations is a technically good product, and a *good* motive is loyalty to the employer. Ethical public relations, then, is simply being loyal to the client or employer's strategic interests or being good at the craft."[53] Although being technically adept is somewhat necessary for the practice of strategic communication, this viewpoint is not helpful in a postmodern moment of narrative contention and metanarrative decline.[54] Instead, IMC scholars and practitioners must seek another path to discovering communication ethics. Ronald C. Arnett, Pat Arneson, and Leeanne M. Bell state, "Negotiating competing social goods is the communicative answer to an era in which there is no 'one' single communication ethic—there are multiple communication ethics."[55]

Carl H. Botan recommends a dialogic approach to strategic communication, instead of one social good of technical competence in service to a client or employer, "Communication ethics from a dialogic perspective is an ongoing negotiation of rival social goods"[56] The dialogic perspective is not centered on relationships; rather, it is grounded in content and learning: "The crucial element of dialogic ethics is the choice to learn; learning requires content—one needs to learn 'something.' The ethical content comes from the narrative structure upon which a person in dialogue stands; dialogue requires one to know one's own position and that of the other person."[57] Arnett et al.'s "dialogic turn" explains the role of communication ethics have in discerning a multiplicity of goods in postmodernity: "The 'dialogic turn' embraces this multiplicity of 'goods,' seeking to meet, learn from, and negotiate with difference. Communication ethics are central to the dialogic process of negotiating contending social goods in a postmodern society, an era of narrative and virtue contention."[58] In keeping with this understanding of the role of communication ethics, the connection between rhetoric and virtue offers a communication ethics position that can assist in negotiating contending social goods in postmodern IMC theory and practice. We can look to rhetorical *phronesis*—"a practical discourse tradition . . . that seeks to mediate between universal truths and the concrete situation"[59] for help to navigate ethical IMC, with the metaphor of *societas* and the metaphor of obligation as two guideposts along the rhetorical approach to IMC.

A Constructive Approach to IMC

In *Built to Last*, James Collins and Jerry Porras discuss "pragmatic idealism" as a result of breaking the "tyranny of the OR." The tyranny of the OR is a kind of false dichotomy that visionary businesses discarded in favor of the "Genius of the AND."[60] The tyranny of the OR forces us to choose sides at moments where choosing a side is the least productive thing we can do. The Genius of the AND is not a relativist acceptance of every idea as good; rather, it allows us to discern multiple helpful and smart approaches to a set of problems. In IMC, integrating the areas of advertising, public relations, marketing communication, and other forms of strategic persuasive communication simply to create a new area of study or to create new turf to be defended is not the aim of this project, nor is it in the minds of scholars and practitioners. The communication discipline has much to offer integrated marketing communication as a theoretical ground for more ethical and effective practice, avoiding unreflective, emotivistic practices. The attractiveness of IMC as a hermeneutic entrance into the challenges of consumption in postmodernity comes not from its status as "the latest fad" but from an enduring appreciation for what it means to be human, in the very human pursuit of the marketplace. We are not silos that divide along camps of advertising and public relations. We are holistic beings who make meaning from symbols, who make sense of our past and lived experiences, and who are made to live and communicate with each other. The metaphor of the Genius of the AND encourages us to seek new ways of meaning not just from the sublime but from the mundane. S. Alyssa Groom writes

> IMC theory and practice must attend to the reality that people do not organize their lives around things; rather they use things to communicate order and organization in their lives, even if only for the sake of appearances. People ascribe to a way of life, not to products and brands. They exchange and use products and brands as ways of associ-

ating with others, challenging IMC to encounter consumers, not just communicate at or with them. IMC must recognize that while cost/benefit assessments no longer define the consumer, the narrative through which he or she seeks to unify meaning and purpose in his or her life does define the consumer.[61]

Understanding IMC as human communication calls for a constructive, humanities-based approach. Arnett and Arneson suggest metaphor as a potential key to understanding:

> Metaphor is a form of linguistic implementation that provides a unique response to a given historical moment, while also being guided by a communicator's narrative framework. Metaphor is a dialogic medium between narrative and historical situation; it points the communicator in a direction that is appropriate for the historical moment, while also being directed by the historical moment.[62]

I suggest two metaphors for understanding IMC: *societas* and obligation.

Metaphors for IMC: *Societas* and Obligation

According to Lee Wilkins and Clifford Christians, "persuasive communication that erodes trust among members of the community or between community members and essential institutions should be considered morally blameworthy. In this sense, selling a product and espousing a particular point of view should not trump essential social connection."[63] I use the term *societas* as a metaphor that calls us to living together with mutual trust as Wilkins and Christians describe. Albert R. Jonsen and Stephen Toulmin explain the ancient Roman concept of a *societas*[64] (a partnership to finance commercial projects was different than a usurious loan[65]), because the *societas* required a burden of risk that the lender and the received both carried. Therefore, it was allowed to collect the profit from this venture. Even St. Thomas Aquinas found this to be an acceptable (i.e., not sinful) form of financial cooperation:

> Aquinas developed the argument: one who commits his money to a joint enterprise does not give up its ownership; he takes the risk of its loss should the enterprise fail. He can take part of the profit that comes from the enterprise because it comes from his own property. Both partners are joint owners; both bear any losses and enjoy any profits.[66]

The metaphor of *societas* encourages organizations and individuals to seek common ground so that trust can be built. Often, the metaphor of *societas* reveals itself in a crisis situation, showing the necessity of fostering trust between organizations and stakeholders. Christine Arena describes the effects of upholding public trust through facing the truth, using the utility company Public Service Company of New Mexico (PNM) as an example.[67] In April 2001, a tiny hole in a gas pipe lead to a major explosion in downtown Santa Fe, seriously injuring one victim and trapping another under building rubble. PNM's response began immediately, and by providing truth and transparency, weathered the crisis and prevailed as a stronger company. For example, PNM held a press conference to announce the findings of the accident investigation, painstakingly illustrating every aspect of the report—much of which showed PNM's negligence prior to the accident. In addition, the company implemented significant improvements to its safety policies, recordkeeping, and communication plans. According to Frederick Bermudez, PNM's director of corporate communications, "Now our standards are far more stringent, our system is safer, and as a whole, we are a more functional organization—all because we admitted fault and faced serious flaws in our system." [68] A commitment to transparency and openness in communication didn't just save the company, it made it stronger than ever.

While the use of rhetoric can be found from micro levels (inter- and intrapersonal communication) to macro levels (political communication or mass communication), the ancient Greek conception of rhetoric in the polis is especially relevant in a postmodern era, with its multiplicity of perspectives, ethics, and competing goods and narratives. Gerard A. Hauser explains rhetoric's importance in this historical moment: "We need competent rhetoric whenever prudent conduct is uncertain. Competent rhetoric is a pluralistic society's best hope for accommodating multiple perspectives through resolute action that serves just ends."[69]

Lee Wilkins and Clifford Christians connect the metaphor of *societas* to our own innate humanity and the humanness of living in society. Violating this through IMC marginalizes humans instead of empowering them: "we argue that our robust concept of humanness embedded in culture as a more vital description of 21st-century humanity, means that activities based on caveat emptor lack moral suasion. We suggest instead a moral model of persuasion based on the notion of empowerment for multiple stakeholders."[70]

Another metaphor, obligation, provides guidance for IMC in the historical moment of the twenty-first-century marketplace. One of the ideas the metaphor of obligation brings forth is the idea of stewardship. Richard John Neuhaus explains the Christian view of the responsibility we have in the marketplace with this term: "A steward is someone who takes care of things, who keeps the household in good order. 'Stewardship' says very nicely what we mean by economic responsibility . . . The Christian who is engaged in economic activity understands that he is responsible to the Ultimate Economist, who is none less than God."[71] Being guided by the metaphor of obligation in IMC is related to this concept of stewardship. We have a responsibility to keep the household in good order—household being part of the Greek root of the word economy.[72] Whether one works from a Judeo-Christian perspective or from a secular humanist perspective, the metaphor of obligation guides us toward being stewards of the household of humanity. Neuhaus, working from the Christian perspective, also sheds light on the difficulties we may have with reconciling economics, the marketplace, and exchange of goods and services with any type of morality or virtue. First, the scope of economics is broad and complex independent of religious or moral truth. Second, because of this complexity, "how on earth can we make religious or moral sense of it? A third reason follows. Because it is so hard to get a handle on economics, and because economic behavior seems to be motivated by base self-interest, the entire subject seems to lack moral dignity."[73]

If we look at the metaphor of obligation in IMC as pointing us toward stewardship, then we have a responsibility to be stewards of our own participation in the marketplace. As Neuhaus states, "The managers of giant transnational corporations may feel that the entire future of humanity depends upon what they do. In the *really* big picture, however, each of us has but a small piece of the action, so to speak. Small does not mean unimportant, however."[74] We must not succumb to routine cynicism about our role in the marketplace because it appears to be a leviathan.[75] Ronald C. Arnett and Pat Arneson explain the potential effects of routine cynicism: "In some cases, cynical evaluations and actions are situationally appropriate. But overall, the cynical wave of looking out for one's own interests, adopting a 'survival mentality' (Lasch 1984, 64) without a commitment to the common good, carves a pathway to social disaster."[76]

Guided by the metaphor of obligation, we can change our response in the face of a vast and complex economy. Jim Collins illustrates of the metaphor of obligation as guiding one person toward excellence in the social sector with the story of Roger Briggs, a young physics teacher at a Colorado suburban public high school:

> As he settled into daily teaching, a persistent thought pushed to the front of his consciousness, like a pebble inside a shoe: *Our schools could be so much better.* But what could he do? He wasn't principal. He wasn't superintendent. He wasn't governor. Roger Briggs wanted to remain on the front line of education, shoulder to shoulder with fellow teachers. After becoming department chair, Briggs decided to turn his little arena into a pocket of greatness. "I rejected the idea of being just a member of the 'working class,' accepting good as good enough. I couldn't change the whole system, but I could change our 14-person science department."[77]

Jim Collins calls this "a culture of discipline." The culture of discipline, combined with an ethic of entrepreneurship, produces greatness.[78] The culture of discipline cannot rely on coercion and power: "If I put a loaded gun to your head, I can get you to do things you might not otherwise do, but I've not practiced leadership; I've exercised power. *True leadership only exists if people follow when they have the freedom not to.* If people follow you because they have no choice, then you are not leading."[79]

James Twitchell connects this type of coercion to a simplistic understanding of the IMC theory of branding. In response to Naomi Klein's critique of branding, which lamented a "fanaticism for homogeneity" approach to keeping a consistent brand message, Twitchell states:

> Klein's concerns are logical if you perceive branding as a one-way, univocal, "yelling down the pipe" kind of communication. If branding is how you stamp the ownership message on the bleating steer, then she is correct. Much as we may comfort ourselves in seeing branding this way (if only because it exonerates us of any responsibility as consumers), such is rarely the case. Commercial narrative, like any kind of storytelling, depends as much on the listener as on the storyteller. The audience is always negotiating meaning, affirming and subverting.[80]

An understanding of branding that absolves us of any responsibility as consumers does not fit into the metaphor of obligation as a guiding concept in IMC. Similarly, the negotiation of meaning of a brand or commercial narrative is a communication activity that requires participation from both parties. The metaphor of obligation includes the ideas of stewardship and the culture of discipline and guides us as consumers and

producers, as buyers and sellers, and as managers and workers, all participating together in the branding narratives of IMC.

Skittles: Excess or Deficiency?

A common phrase in the marketplace is the idea that one can "manage the brand." This top-down managerial approach to brand narratives
undermines the negotiation of meaning that Twitchell suggests. If an organization's primary concern is the control of its brand's meaning for its
consumers, its management spends so much time enforcing its version of
meaning upon its consumers that it loses sight of what the organization
could be. On the opposite end, absconding all responsibility for brand
communication to only consumers is just as problematic. An example of
this was a redesign of the Skittles brand candies'[81] website in 2009. Skittles' agency, Agency.com,[82] created a home page for Skittles' website
that pulled all of its social media feeds from Twitter, Facebook,
YouTube, and Wikipedia so that visitors could see how the brand was
being discussed online in real time. While this approach garnered much
attention in the trade publications such as *Advertising Age* and *PR Week,*
users soon realized that using the word "Skittles" in their tweets or status
updates would get them seen on Skittles' site.

Allyson Kapin of *Fast Company* noted

> Some of the tweets have nothing to do with the actual candy but are us-
> ing the Skittles hashtag to promote their own campaigns or ideas. "Pro
> Iraqi Refugees need your help. Click here to sign the petition: #Skittles.
> [Please RT!)," or "WFMU Fundraising Marathon now underway. Tune
> in: or pledge at wfmu.org #Skittles."[83]

Besides the social justice and philanthropic causes that that capitalized
on Skittles' visibility, Skittles' social media outlets also featured profani-
ty and other questionable content, including racial slurs and pedophilia,[84]
all tagged with the #skittles hash tag, earning its share of ink as the trade
media press questioned the stupidity (giving up "control") and the genius
(a publicity stunt) of the two day free-for-all.[85] Skittles removed the
Twitter feed from prominence on its website, making it a smaller link at
the bottom of the page. One might say that Skittles gave up control of the
brand to its advertising agency, who may have been testing the limits of

this nascent form of integrated marketing communication. Even if the goal for this experiment was press agentry—creating an event that garners press coverage—and this goal was certainly met, the Skittles example demonstrates a need for a constructive approach to IMC and social media, one that relies more on unreflective hype and publicity rather than any content or theory. The Skittles example prompts us to ask questions such as what obligation does Skittles have to its consumers, its shareholders, or its employees? Is using social media in this fashion engaging a sense of *societas* or rejecting it? Is Skittles fashioning its brand narrative online by consuming its consumers' own communication? How are people talking about Skittles online constructing meaning from the symbolic nature of Skittles' online communication?

These questions may not be answerable, but we should be asking these questions. Somewhere between total control and total abdication of a brand and its communication lies the area of moderation—what Aristotle called the Golden Mean, the space between excess and deficiency. This area is where virtue lies.[86] If too much control is excessive, too little responsibility deficient, then how can we practice what Aristotle would call virtuous IMC, especially in the area of social media? In the next chapter I argue that understanding social media as epideictic rhetoric, attending to ethics and decorum, would enable a praxis approach to IMC.

Notes

1. Don E. Schultz, Stanley I. Tannenbaum, and Robert F. Lauterborn, *Integrated Marketing Communications: Putting it Together and Making it Work* (Chicago: NTC Publishing Group, 1993), 13.

2. Don E. Schultz and Philip J. Kitchen, *Communicating Globally: An Integrated Marketing Approach* (Chicago: NTC Publishing Group, 2000), 20-21.

3. Schultz et al. *Integrated Marketing Communications*, 56.

4. Schultz et al. *Integrated Marketing Communications*, 56.

5. Don E. Schultz and Heidi Schultz, *IMC, The Next Generation: Five Steps For Delivering Value and Measuring Financial Returns* (New York: McGraw-Hill, 2004), 86.

6. Schultz and Schultz, *IMC, The Next Generation*, 87.

7. Schultz and Schultz, *IMC, The Next Generation*, 87.

8. Anders Gronstedt, *The Customer Century: Lessons from World Class Companies in Integrated Communications* (New York: Routledge, 2000), 9.

9. Schultz and Schultz, *IMC, The Next Generation*, 87.

10. Philip J. Kitchen and Patrick de Pelsmacker, *Integrated Marketing Communications: A Primer* (New York: Routledge, 2004), 8.

11. Kitchen and de Pelsmacker, *Integrated Marketing Communications*, 11.

12. Joep P. Cornelissen, "Integrated Marketing Communications and the Language of Marketing Development," *International Journal of Advertising* 20(2001), 484.

13. David W. Guth and Charles Marsh, *Public Relations: A Values-Based Approach,* 5th ed. (Boston: Allyn & Bacon, 2012), 11.

14. Schultz and Schultz, *IMC, The Next Generation,* 87.

15. Ronald C. Arnett and Pat Arneson. *Dialogic Civility in a Cynical Age* (Albany, NY: SUNY Press, 1999), 7.

16. Ronald C. Arnett, *Dialogic Confessions: Bonhoeffer's Rhetoric of Responsibility* (Carbondale, IL: Southern Illinois U P, 2005), 2.

17. Tony Proctor and Philip J. Kitchen. "Communication in Postmodern Integrated marketing." *Corporate Communications: An International Journal* 7 (2002), 147.

18. Proctor and Kitchen. "Communication in Postmodern Integrated marketing," 147.

19. Philip J. Kitchen, "The Marketing Communication– A Leviathan Unveiled?" *Marketing, Intelligence and Planning* 12 (1994), 19.

20. Kitchen, "A Leviathan Unveiled?," 12.

21. Kitchen, "A Leviathan Unveiled?," 12.

22. Christopher E. Hackley, and Philip J. Kitchen. "Ethical Perspectives on the Postmodern Communications Leviathan." *Journal of Business Ethics* 20 (1999), 19.

23. Arnett, *Dialogic Confessions,* 270.

24. Arnett, *Dialogic Confessions,* 208.

25. Simon Torp. "Integrated Communications: From One Look to Normative Consistency." *Corporate Communications: An International Journal* 14 (2009), 190.

26. Lars Thøger Christensen, A. Fuat Firat, and Simon Torp. "The Organization of Integrated Communications: Toward Flexible Integration." *European Journal of Marketing* 42(2008), 425.

27. Gerard A. Hauser, *Vernacular Voices: The Rhetoric of Publics and Public Spheres* (Columbia: University of South Carolina Press, 1999), 33.

28. Hauser, *Vernacular Voices,* 32-33.

29. Hauser, *Vernacular Voices,* 33.

30. Hackley and Kitchen, "Ethical Perspectives on the Postmodern Communications Leviathan," 19.

31. J. Michael Sproule, "The New Managerial Rhetoric and the Old Criticism." *Quarterly Journal of Speech* 74(1988), 469

32. Sproule, "The New Managerial Rhetoric," 469.

33. Sproule, "The New Managerial Rhetoric," 484.

34. Robert L. Heath, "A Rhetorical Perspective on the Values of Public Relations: Crossroads and Pathways Toward Concurrence." *Journal of Public Relations Research* 12 (2000), 72.

35. Heath, "A Rhetorical Perspective," 78.

36. Botan, Carl, "A Semiotic Approach to the Internal Functioning of Public: Implications for Strategic Communication and Public Relations." *Public Relations Review* 24(1998), 24.

37. Botan, "A Semiotic Approach," 36.

38. Botan, "A Semiotic Approach," 38.

39. F. Byron Nahser, *Learning to Read the Signs* (Boston: Butterworth-Heinemann, 1997), 80.

40. Proctor and Kitchen, "Communication in Postmodern Integrated Marketing," 151.

41. Proctor and Kitchen, "Communication in Postmodern Integrated Marketing," 151.

42. James E. Grunig, and Larissa A. Grunig. "Toward a Theory of the Public Relations Behavior of Organizations: Review of a Program of Research." *Public Relations Research Annual* 1 (1989), 30.

43. Carl H. Botan. "Ethics in Strategic Communication Campaigns: The Case for a New Approach to Public Relations." *The Journal of Business Communication* 34 (1997), 196.

44. Botan, "Ethics in Strategic Communication," 197.

45. Sid Lowe et al., "The Fourth Hermeneutic in Marketing Theory," *Marketing Theory* 5, no.2 (2005), 198-199.

46. Lowe et al., "The Fourth Hermenutic," 198.

47. Lowe et al., "The Fourth Hermenutic," 199.

48. O.C. Ferrell, Larry G. Gresham, and John Fraedrich. "A Synthesis of Ethical Decision Models for Marketing." *Journal of Macromarketing* 9 (1989), 57.

49. Ferrell et al., 57.

50. R. Eric Reidenbach and Donald Robin. "Some Initial Steps Toward Improving the Measurement of Ethical Evaluations of Marketing Activities." *Journal of Business Ethics* 7, no. 11 (1988), 874-8.

51. Shelby Hunt and Scott Vitell. "A General Theory of Marketing Ethics." *Journal of Macromarketing* 6 (1986), 7.

52. Hunt and Vitell, "A General Theory of Marketing Ethics," 7.

53. Botan, "Ethics in Strategic Communication," 196.

54. Arnett and Arneson, *Dialogic Civility in a Cynical Age,* 62; Arnett, *Dialogic Confessions,* 29-30.

55. Ronald C. Arnett, Pat Arneson, and Leeanne M. Bell. "Communication Ethics: The Dialogic Turn." In *Exploring Communication Ethics: Interviews with Influential Scholars in the Field.* Pat Arneson, ed. (New York: Peter Lang, 2007), 167.

56. Arnett and Arneson. *Dialogic Civility in a Cynical Age,* 166.

57. Arnett and Arneson. *Dialogic Civility in a Cynical Age,* 166.

58. Arnett et al., "The Dialogic Turn," 144.

59. Ronald C.Arnett. "The Status of Communication Ethics Scholarship in Speech Communication Journals from 1915 to 1985." *Central States Speech Journal* 38(1987), 45.

60. James C. Collins and Jerry I. Porrans. *Built to Last: Successful Habits of Visionary Companies* (New York: HarperBusiness-Harper-Collins, 1997), 48.

61. S. Alyssa Groom, "Integrated Marketing Communication Anticipating the 'Age of Engage,' *Communication Research Trends* 7, no. 4 (2008), 15.

62. Arnett and Arneson. *Dialogic Civility in a Cynical Age,* 299.

63. Lee Wilkins and Clifford G. Christians. "Philosophy Meets the Social Sciences: The Nature of Humanity in the Public Arena." *Journal of Mass Media Ethics* 16, no. 2-3 (2001), 108.

64. Jeffrey J. Maciejewski also refers to *societas* as "…the disposition of living with one another in society…" ("Postmodern Rhetoric" 104)

65. Albert Jonsen and Stephen Toulmin, *The Abuse of Casuistry: A History of Moral Reasoning.* (Berkeley and Los Angeles: University of California Press, 1990), 185.

66. Jonsen and Toulmin, *The Abuse of Casuistry,* 185.

67. Christine Arena, *The High Purpose Company* (New York: Collins, 2007), 101-102.

68. Arena, *The High Purpose Company,* 102.

69. Hauser, *Vernacular Voices,* 33.

70. Wilkins and Christians, "Philosophy Meets the Social Sciences," 108.

71. Richard John Neuhaus, *Doing Well & Doing Good: The Challenge to the Christian Capitalist* (New York: Doubleday, 1992), 20.

72. *Oikos* (house) and *nomos* (manager or ruler). Neuhaus, *Doing Well & Doing Good,* 20.

73. Neuhaus, *Doing Well & Doing Good,* 20.

74. Neuhaus, *Doing Well & Doing Good,* 20.

75. Kitchen, "The Marketing Communication– A Leviathan Unveiled?", 23-4.

76. Arnett and Arneson. *Dialogic Civility in a Cynical Age,* 166.

77. Jim Collins, *Why Business Thinking is Not the Answer: Good to Great and the Social Sectors. A Monograph to Accompany Good to Great* (Boulder, CO: Jim Collins, 2005.), 13-14.

78. Jim Collins, *Good to Great: Why Some Companies Make the Leap...and Others Don't* (New York: HarperCollins, 2001), 126.

79. Collins, *Why Business Thinking is Not the Answer,* 12-13.

80. James B. Twitchell, *Branded Nation: The Marketing of Megachurch, College Inc., and Museumworld,* (New York: Simon & Schuster, 2004), 296-297.

81. www.fastcompany.com/blog/allyson-kapin/radical-tech/will-online-social-networks-help-rebuild-skittles-brand

82. www.adweek.com/news/technology/skittles-site-ends-extreme-social-makeover-101491

83. www.fastcompany.com/blog/allyson-kapin/radical-tech/will-online-social-networks-help-rebuild-skittles-brand

84. http://techcrunch.com/2010/02/05/skittles-website/

85. www.businessweek.com/managing/content/mar2009/ca2009038_020385.htm

86. Aristotle, *Nichomachean Ethics* (Oxford: Oxford UP, 1998), 30-31.

Chapter 3
Social Media, IMC, and Rhetorical Decorum

Social Media and Epideictic Rhetoric

In chapter 1 I introduced the idea of social media as epideictic rhetoric, building on Lawrence Rosenfield's assertion[1] that the audience for epideictic rhetoric bears witness more than serving as assessor or critic— roles that more naturally fit with judicial or deliberative rhetoric. An assumption that rhetoric fits neatly into Aristotle's rhetorical settings that correspond to the past, present, and future is in itself unrhetorical. I do not want to dismiss the potential for social media as judicial or deliberative rhetoric; rather, approaching social media as epideictic rhetoric might offer a more robust understanding of this phenomenon. In *The Rhetoric*, Aristotle establishes what epideictic rhetoric aims to do, what audience it serves, and what kinds of arguments and proofs an orator can make in epideictic oratory.[2] He explains that examples are appropriate for deliberative rhetoric, because we judge future events based on what might have transpired in the past, and that enthymeme is suitable for judicial rhetoric, because we have doubts about what might have happened in the past and therefore we have to construct the syllogism to determine "why a thing must have happened or proving it happened."[3] For epideictic oratory, however, heightening of effects is most appropriate, because it "invests deeds with dignity and nobility."[4] It is important that we endow these deeds with the characteristics of dignity and nobility because in a speech that praises "we praise a man for what he has actually done . . . . we must try to prove our hero's acts are intentional."[5] For Aristotle, the

53

action is not enough; the praise (or conversely, the blame) that epideictic rhetoric heaps on a hero or villain must come from the action being a deliberate choice that demonstrates the hero's character. Aristotle's hero cannot just be lucky (although he acknowledges that luck plays a part in our lives); he must be intentional about why he chose to perform these heroic deeds. We can also view this in terms of blame. A tragic accident deserves less blame than a premeditated act based on unvirtuous behavior such as meanness of spirit or cowardice. This intentionality is also seen in the description of Aristotle's *phronimos*: the incarnation of rhetoric, virtue, and *phronesis* in the *phronimos* provides a standard-bearer to whom we can look for guidance. The *phronimos* puts the virtues into practice in real and challenging ethical situations. Lois Self explains, "It is to the *phronimos* that the public should look to for guidance about its general welfare."[6] For Aristotle, the *phronimos*[7] is meant to participate in public life, because he is equipped with all of the qualities that promote excellence in deliberation "to render competent judgments on issues of contingent choice."[8]

Gerard Hauser continues, saying the *phronimos*'s qualities make him the embodiment of the virtue of prudence: "Prudence is an excellence, arête, made visible in a person's capacity to locate the golden mean between the vices of excess and defect. Practical reasoning involves an ability to project the consequences of actions in line with an understanding of other commitments."[9] The *phronimos* and his connection to this virtue make him especially fitting to participate in epideictic rhetoric as a celebration of virtue in a society because of his ethos.

Social Media and the Ethos of Epideictic Rhetoric

As I argued in chapter 1, social media could be a form of epideictic rhetoric because it is simultaneously present and distant, and as Rosenfield offers, can "call upon us to join with our community in giving thought to what we witness."[10] Although the traditional explanation of the epideictic genre is that it works to conserve a society, holding up what is to praise or blame,[11] Dale L. Sullivan presents a more expansive understanding of epideictic, relating to ethos, which makes more connection to how we can use the epideictic genre for more than conservative or instructive purposes. Drawing on Aristotle's claim that the ethos of a speaker inspiring pathos in the audience fit best with epideictic rhetoric, Sullivan elaborates on the aspects of a speaker's ethos that must be present to create "a sense of communion . . . (1) the rhetor's reputation, (2) the rhetor's vision, (3) the rhetor's authority, (4) the rhetor's presentation of good reasons, and (5) the rhetor's creation of consubstantiality with the audience."[12] If social media could be considered a type of epideictic rhetoric, the rhetor and the audience take on responsibility and roles that work together to create this communality. Sullivan outlines each of the five elements of the ethos and how they work to elevate the role of epideictic rhetoric beyond the ceremonial.

The first, the reputation of the rhetor, can reflect an organization or an individual who has some credibility with the audience. The idea of credibility is contested by other users in any given media. For example, international public relations firm Edelman releases the Edelman Trust Barometer[13] every year, surveying 5,075 people in 525 countries on five continents who are aged 18-64, college educated, in the top 25 percent of household income per age group in each country and who "report significant media consumption and engagement in business news and public policy."[14] In the twelfth year of its existence, the Trust Barometer measures levels of trust in organizations across countries and sectors and also measure *who* we trust the most. In 2012, when asked the question "If you heard information about a company from one of these people, how credible would that information be?" 68 percent of participants responded that an academic or expert in the field would be most credible. 38 percent responded that the CEO of a company would be most trusted (fourth on the list), and only 65 percent stated "a person like me" as most credible (holding the seventh out of eight places on the list).[15] Therefore, the CEO of an organization tweeting or Facebooking on behalf of the company is perceived as less credible than an independent expert or academic in the field. This understanding of a rhetor's credibility and its effect on an organization's reputation gains even more weight when combined with the ethos (or shared and implied values) of the audience.

The ethos of the audience also comes into play in the second area of ethos in epideictic—that of a rhetor's vision. Sullivan describes the rhetor's vision as "the audience's recognition that the rhetor (as one who represents the culture) 'sees' reality as the culture sees it, experiences the numinous, meditates upon Being, and is able to evoke the numinous experience through symbol. It is, in short, the recognition of the rhetor's vision or inspiration."[16] The "numinous" to which Sullivan refers is based on Edwyn Robert Bevan's read of Ruldolf Otto's description of this state of mind, which "is a sense of awe or intense admiration that can be evoked through symbols but not through conceptualized statements."[17] The symbolic nature of rhetoric and language, combined with the visual and aural, create opportunities for social media to offer a "numinous" experience. In addition to *amplifying* the culture for the audience (as Aristotle understood epideictic to do), rhetors *mediate* the culture for the audience, interpreting the numinous experience with their reflection of their existence in order to inspire the audience. Sullivan clarifies that while the "inspiration" function may not be acknowledged by all scholars because "this may be characterized as nothing more than the ability to put voice to an interpretation of reality, it has been understood by some to be a form of inspiration, and it is experienced as a sort of unveiling by those who share a less sophisticated version of the same interpretation."[18]

Social Media and Epideictic Rhetoric: Uncovering Being

Returning to the discussion of social media as epideictic rhetoric in chapter 1 and the argument that epideictic rhetoric has the potential for much more than ceremonial praise and blame, Rosenfield argues that epideictic rhetoric is often treated as the mode of rhetoric most relegated to ornament and amusement. While forensic rhetoric metes out justice and deliberative rhetoric can change the course of a nation, limiting epideictic rhetoric's reach to praise and blame shortchanges its true potential as an opportunity for an audience to bear witness to Being.[19] Epideictic rhetoric, according to Rosenfield, relates to *alaetheia*—what he defines as "the unconcealment of things in their 'thisness'"—and *thaumadzein*— "a beholding wonder, an overwhelming sense of exultation that sweeps over us when we catch a glimmer of excellence abiding in a familiar object or event."[20] Rosenfield warns us to avoid the trap of thinking of rhetoric *only* as argumentation, which does not allow for the radiance and wonder that can result from epideictic:

> We can also better understand the Greek stress on rhetoric's sensuality if we temper the association of rhetoric with argumentative debate. The notion of radiance suggests that far from forcing his ideas on an audience with cold logic, the orator charms his listeners; he enchants them so that they, *like him*, are "attracted" to a mode of thinking.[21]

Rosenfield's understanding of epideictic appears to be influenced by the Heideggerian concept of Being and its relationship to communication and rhetoric. In *Being and Time*, Martin Heidegger talks about the Greek notion of *aletheia* as it relates to "Being-true": "one must let them be seen as something unhidden . . . that is, they must be *discovered*. Similarly, 'Being false' . . . amounts to deceiving in the sense of *covering up* [*verdecken*]: putting something in front of something (in such a way as to let it be seen) and thereby passing it off *as* something which it is *not*."[22] The term *aletheia* comes from the Greek word *lethe*: to cover or forget. *Aletheia* means not covering up or uncovering. In the Heideggerian sense, it means disclosing Being.[23] According to Wilhelm S. Wurzer, Heidegger says in his Aristotle lectures[24] that rhetoric is not just poetic elegance but that in rhetoric lay the possibilities of Being with one another. Rhetoric is not mere technique: it always has an ethical content and purpose. Heidegger goes further to say it is a mode of disclosure of Being. Heidegger's view of rhetoric as Being-with-others in authentic participation coincides with Jürgen Habermas' notion of the public sphere but is rooted in the Ancient Greek polis.[25]

Rhetoric has a special political relationship to *Dasein*. *Dasein* and Heidegger's public sphere are understood from standpoint of mood. Speaking about how Heidegger views the ethical—anything that opens to the essence of Being is ethical. According to Wurzer, rhetoric is a mode of truth that helps us to exceed the everyday. It communicates an authenticity of Being linguistically. Rhetoric is an important and essential mode of disclosure that requires implicit awareness of truth. Being is not a human product—it goes beyond beings, and communication is the human expression of Being. Rhetoric has an awakening and transforming function, as opposed to functioning as a simulation, or an empty technique.[26]

Heidegger also distinguishes between *rede* and *gerede*, where *rede* is communication ("talk") and *gerede* is idle talk, or gossip. *Rede* helps to uncover Being while *gerede* conceals it; engaging in *gerede* moves humans away from Being. Heidegger laments the casual discourse that becomes "fashionable" as idle talk because it lessens Being: "just as it was an open question whether those who talked of 'lived experience' still in fact had the possibility to 'experience' anything, or whether this possibility was rather not exhausted precisely because idle talk about it had begun. Catchwords and catchphrases are indices of idle talk, which is a mode of being of *Dasein* in the Anyone."[27]

Heidegger's description of idle talk (*gerede*) sounds very descriptive of a viral meme in social media. After all, the Lolcat[28] phenomenon found on www.icanhazcheeseburger.com (where cute photos of cats are captioned, usually in a font called "Impact," in an imagined cat dialect) is an excellent example of idle talk in social media—it exists for pure entertainment. However, Heidegger doesn't want to eliminate idle talk; instead, he sees that idle talk offers the prospect for *Dasein* because it potentially grows into an opportunity that promotes understanding: "This possibility of genuinely entering into the discourse nevertheless exists and is documented especially in this, that the discoveredness which is given with a word can be rectified with certain sentences and developed further. Indeed, articulated discourse can help first by grasping possibilities of being for the first time which before were already always experienced implicitly . . . Thus discourse, especially poetry, can even bring about the release of new possibilities of the being of *Dasein*. In this way, discourse proves itself positively as a *mode of maturation, a mode of temporalization* of *Dasein* itself." *Dasein* is Heidegger's term meaning "Being-There," and it describes his philosophy of "being-in-the-world; or as Michael J. Hyde describes this relationship of communication to Being: "The human world is only possible through our use of language, which 'presences' Being."[29] Therefore, discourse as a mode of temporalization situates us in the present, relying again on the etymology of epideictic: "Phenomenologically speaking, truth happens, first and foremost, as an act of disclosure, a 'showing forth' (*epi-deixis*) or epideictic display of something that presents itself to us. The assertion and validity of any 'truth-claim' presupposes the occurrence of such an act."[30] Based on this understanding of epideictic as showing forth, social media could be considered a form of epideictic in that it reveals the complexity of everyday life that always existed but is now disclosed through a different medium.

Social Media as Epideictic Rhetoric: Celebrating Everyday Life

Examining the interpretations of epideictic rhetoric allows us to engage social media at much more than face value. Rosenfield points us toward the transcendent possibility of epideictic rhetoric that arises from the mundane and routine: "Ordinary events conceal the aura of their being because in our concern for our projects we remain largely unmindful of them. But those who are open to the wonder of what is, in the very fact that it is, may be arrested by some particular of everyday life when they detect in it an indication of the ground from which springs all reality. And that realization, encapsulated in language, will bring forth a sense of gratitude in the witness, an intoxicating reverence for our own human *being* which the observer may feel impelled to share with the community."[31]

The volume of social media that is generated by users documenting their everyday life is significant; as of June 2012, Twitter alone has over 400 million tweets per day.[32] Many of these musings, enabled by smartphone, tablet, and computer usage, could be criticized as trivial. However, the everydayness of Twitter and Facebook make it much more than an aggregate of pet posts, snarky comments, and celebrity gossip—these services document our everyday lives. Even without an account, one can look at Twitter's trending topics to see what a subset of the population is talking about at any given moment. The attention to life's everyday practices, even the most mundane, are described in Michel de Certeau, Luce Giard, and Pierre Mayol's study of a neighborhood in Lyon, France, called "The Practices of Everyday Life." In *Volume 2, Living and Cooking*, de Certeau and his team focus on the more traditionally feminine roles of shopping, cooking, cleaning, and leisure, and how these roles and everyday practices shape society. Observing the interplay of the neighborhood and its inhabitants, Pierre Mayol writes:

> The neighborhood is a dynamic notion requiring a progressive apprenticeship that grows with the repetition of the dweller's body's engagement in public space until it exercises a sort of appropriation of this space. The everyday banality of this process, shared among all urbanites, renders invisible its complexity as a cultural practice and its urgency in satisfying the *urban* desire of dwellers of the city.[33]

Mayol continues, describing the ongoing tension between the private space of the home and the public space of the city as constitutive of the neighborhood that connects these two spaces:

> The neighborhood is the middle term in an existential dialectic (on a personal level) and a social one (on the level of a group of users), between *inside* and *outside*. And it is in the tension between these two terms, an *inside* and an *outside*, which little by little becomes the continuation of an inside, that the appropriation of space takes place. As a result, the neighborhood can be called an outgrowth of the abode; for

the dweller, it amounts to the sum of all trajectories inaugurated from the dwelling place.[34]

Mayol describes the neighborhood as a "possibility offered to everyone"; similarly, the online space of social media is informed by the tension between public and private spaces to construct a similar possibility for everyone. To be clear, however, we have to remember that social media is not "everyone"—it is a space that requires access via technology and infrastructure. "Everyone" is not actually everyone; it is everyone who is privileged to have this access. Nevertheless, Mayol describes a possibility to participate in epideictic rhetoric as Rosenfield theorizes it, especially in viewing glimpses of being in our everyday lives and practices. The mundane social media update of "just made breakfast for my family" promotes a common ground in a virtual neighborhood. This possibility also extends beyond the everydayness of life; it reminds us that we are "dwelling together."

An example of epideictic in everyday lives and how our everyday practices can change the narrative of a community comes from Robert Putnam, who argues "social capital" is generated by participation together in society: "Social capital refers to networks of social connection—doing *with*. Doing good *for* other people, however laudable, is not part of the *definition* of social capital."[35] The everydayness of participating in daily practices together forms social capital that builds community. The title of Putnam's book describing the decline of social capital, *Bowling Alone*, refers to the decline of bowling league participation in American communities as a symptom of this decline. Bowling is not glamorous, nor thrilling, nor unusual, but bowling in a league with friends and neighbors on a weekly league night reinforced social capital. The decline of this routine activity speaks to a much larger problem and demonstrates the importance of dwelling together in everyday life. Putnam gives another example that highlights the importance of small, everyday activities (visits to neighbors) as making or breaking a community. In Providence, Rhode Island, Jewish community members traditionally visited each other with food and pastries to commemorate the holiday of Purim. These visits were part of the Jewish commandment of doing good deeds—called *mitzvahs*—which also contributed to the social capital of the community. What has evolved because of busy lives, Putnam claims, is a donation to charity in the name of the neighbor that replaces the visit and pastries. Putnam states "The philanthropic purpose is admirable. The traditional visits, however, also reinforced bonds within this community. A check in an envelope, no matter how generous, cannot have that same effect."[36]

Doing *with* is part of the mindful participation in the community—our dwelling together. Although doing good *for* other people is still beneficial, according to Putnam, the doing *with* actually has a greater effect on the interconnectivity of humans and institutions. What was a community that centered on doing *with* made a shift to doing *for.* In dwelling together, epideictic rhetoric simultaneously attends to the routine of everyday life, but also to significant or historic events, as I show in the next section.

Social Media as Epideictic Rhetoric: Bearing Witness

According to Rosenfield, bearing witness is a powerful aspect of epideictic rhetoric. One of most significant pieces of epideictic rhetoric in U.S. history is Abraham Lincoln's Gettysburg Address dedicating part of the battlefield as a cemetery in Gettysburg, Pennsylvania. Lincoln acknowledges that while it is important to be in attendance, no action or speech by any of the living could replace or even approach the consecration of the soldiers who had died on the battlefield.[37] In a similar sense, the funeral orations and essays that Jacques Derrida delivered in honor of his friends, including Roland Barthes, Michel Foucault, and Emmanuel Levinas, are striking pieces of epideictic not just because of the stature of his subjects but because of his attentiveness to epideictic as ethical response.[38] According to Brooke Rollins, Derrida understood the paradox of trying to honor the deceased without appropriating the other: "It is the very sanctity of this occasion that makes the funeral speech such a conventional form, one in which words can never do justice to the friend who has died . . . [Derrida's] protestations foreground the ethical problems that presences poses for epideictic oratory. The questions posed when composing an epideictic speech thus become questions of ethical response: *What might I say that will not encroach upon the other? How might I find the words to do justice to this otherness?*"[39] Derrida is so concerned that he will appropriate the other to his own ends in a relationship that is at the same time present and distant, but the alternative—not speaking at all—is even worse. In the end, Rollins argues, "The epideictic orator, then, can never claim to know the deceased, regardless of how intimate the pair was in life . . . . what Derrida's speeches do, however, is allow us to respond to our dead friends, now figured as collections of images that we can visualize and mobilize, while still leaving them to their infinite otherness.[40] We gather to hear a funeral eulogy and pay our respects to the departed at a funeral because we are bearing witness to the impact that the departed left on our lives. Social media is also there but not there—present but distant—at the same time, and as such we have to be concerned, as Derrida was, with appropriating the other for our own ends. Social media lends itself to what Rollins refers to as the "collection of images we can visualize and mobilize" because of the images, text, video, and audio that can live on in the virtual world after the subject has departed the material world. It makes social media an especially appropriate medium for bearing witness, but even so, we must remember that we must try not to appropriate the other for our own ends, and even as we try, Derrida warns us that that we will inevitably fail.

An example of social media as bearing witness and the challenges that presents is the Kony 2012 campaign. In March 2012, one of the topics trending online was "Kony 2012." This online campaign for The Invisible Children non-profit organization seeks to bring Joseph Kony to justice by bringing his crimes (described in the documentary *The Invisible Children*) to light. The documentary describes Kony as a Ugandan ringleader who has actively abducted young children for his guerilla army. The Kony 2012 campaign and movement asks users to retweet and repost the Stop Kony 2012 message so that pressure from the international community will force his arrest and trial. What distinguishes Kony 2012 from previous online awareness campaigns is that the originators are asking users to bear witness through their social networks, knowing that the audience cannot be in Uganda to bear witness physically, but bear witness virtually. The Kony 2012 campaign is an example of epideictic rhetoric that could potentially reflect this reverence for Being that Rosenfield refers to, moving observers to share with a community. The campaign is also an example of Derrida's problem: how can a distance, created by infinite otherness, ever be bridged? The Kony 2012 campaign enjoyed a spike in March 2012 but by April had declined for a few reasons including the personal legal troubles of its producer. It also failed because the population of Uganda is not one homogenous unit: the people of Uganda had mixed feelings and opinions about the point of view that the documentary presented. In addition, the filmmaker was advancing an agenda that did not necessarily align with that of citizens of the countries affected by Joseph Kony's actions, resulting in the sentiment that the documentary was paternalistic and colonializing.[41] That being said, the effort to communicate about a problem that very few people in the United States knew about before the social media campaign demonstrates a strong possibility for social media as epideictic rhetoric that bears witness. Attentiveness to what Derrida calls "the ethics of otherness" and to Rollins' claim that "epideictic rhetoric is always in response"[42] would provide a reflective and constructive orientation to social media as epideictic rhetoric that bears witness.

To be clear, social media can function in forms other than epideictic rhetoric. However, an understanding of social media as a form of epideictic rhetoric can open up the theory and practice of social media in more ethical and productive ways. In a similar manner, the idea of decorum in rhetorical contexts offers a potentially productive approach to social media that allows for differences in audience, speaker, content, and purpose.

Social Media and Epideictic Rhetoric: Educating on Shared Virtue?

Epideictic rhetoric's focus on praise and blame within the present moment has connected it to teaching and educating a people about what their society holds as virtuous. Celeste Michelle Condit positions this characteristic of epideictic into one of the three "functional pairs" she establishes to describe epideictic fully. The first, definition and understanding functions, serves the speaker's purpose when explaining a problem within the context of the audience's shared beliefs. The second, sharing and shaping community, serves to unite and educate the audience around a shared experience. The third, display and entertainment, shows the speaker's ability for eloquence, and entertains while allowing the audience to imagine possibilities.[43]

Condit contends that sharing and shaping community results from the human desire to share community: "Because humans are symbol-creators, they need forms of symbolic sharing. A sense of community is developed and maintained in large part through public speaking and hearing of the community heritage and identity."[44] A community must establish its identity and heritage prior to coming together in this symbolic sharing.

With this understanding of the importance of epideictic rhetoric from multiple perspectives, how do social capital-building examples of epideictic rhetoric emerge in a community? To begin, a story shared by members of a community can actually be understood as beginning "with a speech act that is tested by people and competing world views, then is fashioned into a story with main characters, a history, and a direction"[45] In this way, the stories and narratives that communities forge from deliberation and mutual understanding move into the realm of epideictic.

Mary M. Keys describes the U.S. celebration of Thanksgiving as this type of narrative, growing from the Pilgrims at Plymouth to George Washington's proclamation of a day of gratitude (epideictic rhetoric) to Abraham Lincoln's executive order recognizing it as a holiday (more epideictic rhetoric). Thanksgiving emerged from a virtue (gratitude), "grew into a customary part of a people's way of life, inspired by an especially significant manifestation of this virtue . . . a primarily New England Puritan celebration gradually became recognized as an *American* holiday . . . the family is definitely the prime locus of this element of moral and civic education."[46]

Not only does epideictic foster the symbolic sharing of community, but it also instills and emphasizes those virtues that we hold as a society. Epideictic serves a conservative function: to preserve the virtues that we have publicly agreed upon. In addition, we use these epideictic opportunities to introduce and educate a culture about virtuous and non-virtuous behavior. In the Thanksgiving example, preschool children learn the story of the first Thanksgiving; as they grow older, they learn the virtue of gratitude through the repetition of the story and reflection on what they are grateful for. The Thanksgiving narrative, retold in a public space and then reproduced at home in private, functions as epideictic rhetoric that reinforces the American virtue of gratitude.

The heading for this section contained a question mark. Can social media perform this educative function of epideictic rhetoric? The interpretations of social media as a form of epideictic, uncovering Being, bearing witness, and celebrating everyday life—can this extend to truly serving the function that Aristotle initially described—holding up exemplars that embody the virtues, so that we as a culture can learn and replicate? I argue that yes, social media can achieve this lofty purpose when it reinforces societal norms, and when its users exhibit rhetorical decorum, which reflects the norms of a society. Thomas B. Ferrell, in his study of the rhetorical norms of a culture, describes this connection between norms, rhetorical constraints, and propriety that is evident in Aristotle's rhetorical theory: "it is clear that the speaker and the audience are each regarded as moral agents, bound together in a relationship of civic friendship, in which each party is accountable to the other and to the common good. For Aristotle, then, the ethical domain of our rhetorical norms derives from the situatedness of praxis in a culture. To do what is proper in this ethical sense is to do and respond to what we are called on to do, in character and in response to the recurring restraints of rhetorical settings."[47]

With an understanding of the possibility of social media as epideictic in place, I now turn to Cicero for the conception of decorum that rhetoric espouses and promotes.

Cicero, Decorum, and Rhetoric

Cicero outlines the specifics of decorum in Book III of his earlier work *De Oratore,* but he is more instructive on the relationship between decorum and rhetoric in Book I, where he argues for elevation of rhetoric to an art. Cicero attends to the tension between style and substance that informs rhetorical theory from the pre-Socratics with care, because it is here that he explains the connection between wisdom and eloquence. He gives good reasons for why we should try to be better orators and why being wise and eloquent is a challenge for all humans, even those who speak well.

Cicero explains that while no one can force an audience to sit through a terribly acted play, the courts can force an audience to listen to a poorly given speech:

> For there are no lawsuits or contentions to compel mankind to sit through bad acting on the stage, as they would bear with indifferent oratory in Court. Therefore our orator must carefully see to it, that he not only contents those whom it necessary to satisfy, but is wonderful as well in the eyes of such as have the right to judge freely.[48]

As a result, the onus is squarely on the speaker for the style and substance of the speech. Cicero notes that this is no small feat; it is nerve wracking for the speaker to prepare because of the potential for failure in content, in delivery, and in reception, and it only gets worse as the orator becomes more skilled. "For the better the orator, the more profoundly is he frightened of the difficulty of speaking, and of the doubtful fate of a speech, and of the anticipations of the audience."[49] Cicero is warning his audience that *good* rhetoric is difficult to achieve. Good orators know the power and potential that they hold when they speak and what the consequences are from a poor performance.

Cicero continues to expound on why the stakes are higher for the orator than for others. The first is because rhetoric can cause an undesired action—as Cicero puts it, "they were justifiably fearful, lest what could possibly happen sometime should actually happen then"—and this potential for real action soaks the orator with the cold water of reality.[50] Rhetoric moves language into action. Rhetoric deals in contingency in a particular moment. Cicero knew that the consequences for oratory that actually moved its audience to action could sometimes be unforeseen by the speaker and could last long after the orator ceased to speak. This second reason good orators might quake at the thought of speaking to an audience is because of the longevity of their words and the impact they have on their reputations. For one, the orator does not get the same benefit of the doubt that an actor does. Cicero claims that a poor performance by an actor or musician can be attributed to illness, poor humor, or another excusable condition, "whereas, if it is an orator's shortcoming that is being criticized the same is thought due to stupidity."[51] Not only is stupidity inexcusable, but one mistake can cost an orator his reputation: "For judgment is passing upon us as often as we speak; moreover one mistake in acting does not instantly convict a player of ignorance of acting, but an orator, censured on some point of speaking, is under an established suspicion of dullness once for all, or at any rate for many a day."[52]

From De Oratore *to* Orator

Cicero's description of decorum in *De Oratore* predates his elaboration on decorum and eloquence in *Orator*. Cicero then establishes decorum's relationship to rhetoric in *Orator*: "Discretion, therefore, is the basis of Eloquence, as well as of every other accomplishment. For, as the conduct of life, so in the practice of Speaking, nothing is more difficult than to maintain a propriety of character. This is called by the Greeks [Greek: to prepon], *the becoming*, but we shall call it *decorum;* a subject which has been excellently and very copiously canvassed, and richly merits our attention."[53] Cicero goes on to describe all of the possibilities of what is becoming versus unbecoming. Elaine Fantham highlighted the section that these passages come from in the *Orator* as one of Cicero's most significant to his rhetorical theory because of two reasons: first, he relates the grand/middle/low rhetorical styles to the functions of rhetoric and the artistic appeals of ethos, pathos, and logos; and second, he synthesizes the two Roman meanings of decorum that the Greeks grouped under one, *prepon*.

Michael Leff also argues that with this move—linking the rhetorical styles to the form and subject—Cicero elevates decorum into three roles that move from the exterior to the intrinsic. The first is accommodation to circumstances (such as audience—an exterior orientation); the second, a mediated link between form and context (which moves more inward) and finally, the third, as an organizing principle (most intrinsic). The table below shows the relationship decorum has with form, content and subject:

Purpose	To prove	To please	To sway
Appeal/Content	Logos	Ethos	Pathos
Style/Decorum	Plain style	Middle style	Grand style

Cicero emphasizes the appropriateness of the style to the content of the speech: "He then is truly an Orator (I again repeat it) who can speak upon trivial subjects with simplicity, upon indifferent ones with moderation, and upon weighty subjects with energy and *pathos*."[54] Knowing when to speak on which subjects using the appropriate style gives the Orator an edge not only in speaking publically but in having a successful life.

Cicero's five canons order the aspects of successful speeches: invention, arrangement, style, memory, and delivery. As part of the canon of style, decorum seems, in this order, to be included *after* invention. However, Cicero[55] talks about the relationship between invention and style and makes a significant move from decorum being separated from invention, and with this move, "style is now as much implicated with the subject as is argument."[56]

Since style and invention are so intimately connected, Leff explains, Cicero's elaboration on wisdom and eloquence in *De Oratore* can be related to decorum as well, since Cicero believes that "thought and language work cooperatively as they blend within the texture of a discourse.

This interaction yields a representation of the subject, and a representation achieves decorum by reference to the nature of the subject itself."[57] Cicero's claim that the ideal orator has wisdom and eloquence speaks not just to his ability to manipulate style but to see decorum as a necessity for living the good life: "For [Cicero], propriety or decorum was not only the central concern in rhetoric, but it also functioned as a guiding principle in ethics."[58]

Cicero situated decorum as a much bigger piece of rhetorical theory than mere ornamentation; however, history and purpose have combined to return rhetoric to an ornamental focus. It is this focus that leads to the modernist assumption that decorum is all about bowing to appearance with a subtext of conformity. To which, yes, if decorum only meant appearance, then it could be dismissed as mere ornament. This assumption is problematic for two reasons: one, decorum in its Ciceronian conception is a much more nuanced and complex than mere ornament, and two, etiquette and manners are more than "mere ornament"—they establish a common ground between two people who have very different views. The rules that govern parliamentary procedure (Robert's Rules of Order are the most prevalent) are in place not for conformity but to keep a level of civility when dealing with heated subjects and to expedite decision-making processes that might otherwise end in stalemate. Even a person with a rudimentary understanding of Robert's Rules of Order knows, after attending one meeting run in this fashion, that speaking when another person has the floor, speaking without being recognized by the chair, and speaking for an hour on one topic is not only rude but detrimental to the proceedings and the speaker's own reputation. Although these rules can also be used to enforce conformity and adherence to the majority rule, ultimately, they serve to remind participants of their common ground and prevent descent into confusion and potential violence.

Decorum in the School of Civic Rhetoric:
The Renaissance Humanists

Through a liberal arts education described by Giambattista Vico, the public would understand why providing real evidence in support of an argument is a valid and sound way to engage in public discourse. Supplementing the Greek understanding of rhetoric, the later rhetoricians Quintilian and Cicero added even more of a moral aspect to rhetoric. According to Aristotle, rhetoric is about discerning the good through speaking well and speaking the truth.[59] Cicero adds that eloquence in rhetoric provides a man with a means to "serve the highest interests of mankind."[60] Cicero values an ethical view of rhetoric above law and philosophy.

In his discussion of Ciceronian decorum in Renaissance Humanist rhetoric, James S. Baumlin explains the importance of decorum in this approach to rhetoric:

> A major issue occupying the speakers in *De Oratore* is thus the problem of requisite knowledge. Whereas Cicero's Crassus argues for wide, nearly universal knowledge (thereby wedding rhetoric and philosophy), Antonius limits the orator's scope (1.48-54) emphasizing popular belief, conventional morality, and the techniques of persuasion per se. While Renaissance Humanists continue this debate, their "rhetoric of prudence" typically sought out the more practical knowledge suited to oratory, as Antonius advised, the sort aiding in public deliberation, prudent choice, and civic action. Hence, decorum, at once the capstone of ethics and rhetoric, becomes "a universal rule, in oratory as in life."[61]
>
> The paradox of decorum is that it is universal but specific, according to Baumlin: "The observance of decorum is thus 'universal,' and yet its specific expression continually changes, since 'propriety' is what is fitting and agreeable to an occasion or person [*decree quasi aptum esse consentaneumque temporis et personae*]."[62]

Baumlin highlights decorum's dependence on the audience:

> The fact is that decorous (or indecorous) speech and behavior is necessarily judged after the fact, based on an audience's immediate, concrete response. And while a speaker may predict an audience's response, one can never guarantee that any behavior will yield its desired results. For all the concern theorists show in observing decorum, no one articulates rules sufficient to govern its effective use.[63]

In other words, the members of an audience may not know the particular rules of decorum, but they certainly know then they are violated *and* they are quick to react to a violation.

Decorum in Postmodernity

The interpretations of decorum since Cicero defined it have waxed and waned over two thousand years. In postmodernity, a time of contested narratives and metanarrative decline,[64] a call to decorum might sound obsolete or even worse, hegemonic. However, in his scholarship on Cicero and decorum, Michael Leff rescues decorum from an antiquated instrument of conformity to become a tool for understanding human communication, behavior, and action. Leff describes the necessity to join context and content to propel appropriate action and recognizes how decorum is not grounded in specific rules—this is decorous, that is not—which makes it more robust. Decorum is "the point at which thought and action, form and content, wisdom and eloquence coalesce."[65] In addition, similar to Condit's assessment of epideictic rhetoric as negotiating a form that is both audience- and speaker-centered, the relationship between audience and aesthetics generates a tension between these two meanings of decorum that presents a "productive complication" according to Leff's interpretation of Cicero's vision of decorum it in the Orator.[66]

Second, Leff espouses a workable understanding of decorum, because he believes we need a space between pure opinion and pure science that is "neighborly"—i.e., a space for rhetoric—especially in postmodernity.[67] His use of the metaphor of neighborhood calls to the epideictic function of rhetoric that establishes common ground for the inhabitants of a shared community. De Certeau et al.'s study of an actual neighborhood focuses on propriety as a way of living together; even the vegetable sellers' double entendres (used when describing their wares to female customers) push boundaries of propriety to enliven everyday activities.[68] Their discourse inhabits a space between complete stranger and intimate family member—the neighborly space that Leff might call the space for rhetoric.

Finally, Leff describes an aspect of decorum in postmodernity that particularly applies to epideictic rhetoric:

> From this perspective, propriety no longer appears as captive within the functional pole of an abstract dichotomy between form and function; it becomes a flexible principle that coordinates particular discourses as they simultaneously build internal coherence, refer to a context of facts and circumstances, and stretch outward to alter perception of that context.[69]

This speaks to the function of epideictic rhetoric that encourages its audience to see possibilities that arise from shared experience. Ideally, decorum provides a harmony to the narratives of a culture, foregrounding common ground and a shared future while acknowledging its differences. This is a challenge for any speaker, but finding the right time, place, manner, and content relies on a transcendent coming together of decorum and kairos in epideictic rhetoric.

Decorum and Kairos in Epideictic Rhetoric

The Greek concept that Cicero refers to as a synonym to decorum is *prepon*, but Cicero's decorum, while similar, includes aspects of the Greek idea of *kairos*, or the opportune moment: "Though Latin decorum specifically translates the Greek *to prepon,* it would appear that Ciceronian theory combines *to prepon* with *to kairos*, 'the fitting' and 'the timely' in a complex synthesis, at once observing both the formal and the temporal or situational aspects of discourse."[70] The timing of rhetoric is just as important as the content and manner in which it is presented, and these aspects are equally important to the content of the speech itself. Decorum and *kairos* also function epistemologically as the rhetorical process moves an audience to action: "It is the principle of decorum that allows us to comprehend a situation as a whole, to locate its meaning within a context, and to translate this understanding into a discursive form that becomes an incentive to action."[71] Although the process that brings about future action is in the area of deliberative rhetoric, the incentive to action that Leff refers to can bring together decorum, kairos, and epideictic. An example of this is Jefferson Davis' resignation speech to the Senate on the eve of the Civil War and the Confederate States' secession from the Union, according to Jarrod Atchison. In this example, decorum and timing in epideictic rhetoric allowed Davis to change the terms of the debate over secession and turns the idea that epideictic is only to preserve the status quo on its head. Atchison describes the sophisticated moves that Davis's skill as an orator allow him to make in order to pave the way for future action—the splitting of the Union:

> Decorum, for Davis, was not just being polite to the people who may
> become his enemy. Decorum, for Davis, was a model of interaction that
> he desperately needed his Union counterparts to follow if he was going

to buy time for the burgeoning Confederacy . . . Davis sought to establish that his resignation and secession were the appropriate responses of civilized people. Through Davis's address we gain a more complex understanding of the theoretical functions of decorum, which is sometimes reduced to a restraining force. Instead of simply conceiving of decorum as a stylistic form or a model of interaction that inhibits certain types of utterances, Davis's resignation address demonstrates that decorum can function to broaden a rhetor's options in a tumultuous environment. In this instance, Davis was able to use the decorum surrounding the epideictic nature of the occasion and the timing of the event to circumvent the debate over the legitimacy of secession.[72]

As Atchison argues, Davis appeals to the decorum of the Senate—a common ground—in order to establish that the southern states had to secede because of the *lack* of common ground. In this case, decorum helps Davis to subvert the status quo, not to preserve it. Rosteck and Leff describe how Kenneth Burke, in his description of propriety in *Permanence and Change*, argues that because a speaker privileges his or her perspective, propriety can actually subvert and then reconstruct a text.[73] This is what Davis does in privileging his perspective—that resignation and secession is a necessary act—while appealing to the very decorum and shared ground that allows him to make this argument. To claim that decorum is only superficial ornament denies its potency. In Chapter 5, this important relationship between time, place, manner, and content is situated in the context of free speech and how this might affect social media—and how decorum can guide us through these areas.

Possibilities for Social Media

Social media allows humans to communicate from the trivial to the sublime. No hard and fast rules govern its usage; no Terms of Usage state "You must only tweet about Being!" It makes for a moving target. Decorum fits this moving target because it shows those same qualities. As Leff states, "Decorum has no substantive stability across situations, since it represents a constantly moving process of negotiation. It is, as Trimpi says, 'an activity, rather than a possession, of the consciousness . . .' At the global level, decorum is pure process, but its local manifestations are products that display a powerful solidity."[74] In the next chapters, I will address the global and local manifestations of decorum that can point us to an understanding of social media in an organizational context.

Notes

1. Lawrence W. Rosenfield, "The Practical Celebration of Epideictic," in *Rhetoric in Transition: Studies in the Nature and Uses of Rhetoric*, ed. Eugene E. White (University Park: Pennsylvania State University Press, 1980): 10.

2. Aristotle, *The Rhetoric*, Trans. W.R. Roberts, *The Rhetoric and Poetics of Aristotle* (New York: Modern Library, 1954): 30-35.

3. Aristotle, *The Rhetoric*, 30-35.

4. Aristotle, *The Rhetoric*, 30-35.

5. Aristotle, *The Rhetoric*, 20-25.

6. Lois Self, "Rhetoric and Phronesis: the Aristotelian Ideal," *Philosophy and Rhetoric* 12 (1979): 138.

7. I refer to the male *phronimos* that Aristotle describes; Lois Self explains her position on using only masculine references as follows: "I wish to note that while the usual rendering of *'phronimos'* as 'man of practical wisdom' will be followed herein (since Aristotle obviously would have included only male persons in the category), I find the assumption that phronesis (prudence) is a virtue of only one gender both unfortunate and irrational." Self, "Rhetoric and Phronesis: the Aristotelian Ideal," 144.

8. Rosenfield, "The Practical Celebration of Epideictic," 10.

9. Gerard A. Hauser, "Aristotle on Epideictic: The Formation of Public Morality." *RSQ: Rhetoric Society Quarterly* 29, no. 1 (1999): 13.

10. Rosenfield, "The Practical Celebration of Epideictic," 10.

11. Aristotle, *The Rhetoric*, 15-20.

12. Dale L. Sullivan, "The Ethos of Epideictic Encounter," *Philosophy and Rhetoric* 26, no. 2 (1993): 113-33.

13. "Infographic (Trust in Media)," *Edelman Trust Barometer*, http://trust.edelman.com/trust-download/infographic-trust-in-media/ (accessed March 8, 2013).

14. "Infographic (Trust in Media)," *Edelman Trust Barometer*.

15. "Edelman Trust Barometer Executive Summary," *Edelman Trust Barometer*, http://trust.edelman.com/trust-download/executive-summary/ (accessed March 8, 2013).

16. Sullivan, *The Ethos of the Epideictic Encounter*, 122.

17. Sullivan, *The Ethos of the Epideictic Encounter*, 122.

18. Sullivan, *The Ethos of the Epideictic Encounter*, 122.

19. Rosenfield, "The Practical Celebration of Epideictic," 135.

20. Rosenfield, "The Practical Celebration of Epideictic," 137-38.

21. Rosenfield, "The Practical Celebration of Epideictic," 139.

22. Martin Heidegger, *Being and Time,* John Macquarries and Edward Robinson eds. (New York: Harper & Row, 1962), 56-57.

23. Heidegger, *Being and Time*, 56.

24. According to Ewen, "Hiding behind a bland title is one of Heidegger's most remarkable courses . . . This course, *Basic Concepts of Aristotelian Philosophy,* or, as it is listed in some places, *Aristotle's Rhetoric."* Stuart Ewen, "Reading Logos as Speech:

Heidegger, Aristotle and Rhetorical Politics," *Philosophy and Rhetoric* 38, no. 4 (2005): 288.

25. Heidegger, *Being and Time,* 174.

26. Wilhelm S. Wurzer, "Nietzsche's Return to an Aesthetic Beginning," *Man and World* 11, no. 1-2 (1978): 59-77.

27. Martin Heidegger, *History of the Concept of Time: Prolegomena* (Bloomington, IN: Indiana University Press, 1992), 272.

28. LOL= laugh out loud.

29. Michael J. Hyde, "Searching for Perfection," in *Perspectives on Philosophy of Communication,* Pat Arneson, ed. (West Lafayette, IN: Purdue University Press, 2007), 23.

30. Hyde, "Searching for Perfection," 23.

31. Rosenfield, "The Practical Celebration of Epideictic," 138-39.

32. "Twitter Now Seeing 400 Million Tweets Per Day, Increased Mobile Ad Revenue, Says CEO," *AllTwitter,* http://www.mediabistro.com/alltwitter/twitter-400-million-tweets (accessed March 8, 2013).

33. Michel de Certeau, Luce Giard and Pierre Mayol, *The Practices of Everyday Life, Vol. 2: Living and cooking* (Minneapolis: University of Minnesota Press, 1998) 11.

34. Certeau, Giard and Mayol, *The Practices of Everyday Life,* 11.

35. Robert. D. Putnam, *Bowling Alone: The Collapse and Revival of American Community* (New York: Simon & Schuster, 2000), 117.

36. Putnam, *Bowling Alone,* 116.

37. "Gettysburg Address—'Nicolay Copy,'" *myLOC,* http://myloc.gov/Exhibitions/gettysburgaddress/exhibitionitems/Pages/Transcription.aspx?ex=1@d6d b09e6-d424-4113-8bd2-c89bd42b1fad@1&asset=d6db09e6-d424-4113-8bd2-c89bd42 b1fad:4ab8a6e6-eb9e-40f8-9144-6a417c034a17:13 (accessed March 8, 2013).

38. Brooke Rollins, "The Ethics of Epideictic Rhetoric: Addressing the Problem of Presence through Derrida's Funeral Orations," *Rhetoric Society Quarterly* 35, no. 1 (2005): 12-13.

39. Rollins, "The Ethics of Epideictic Rhetoric," 12-13.

40. Rollins, "The Ethics of Epideictic Rhetoric," 14-15.

41. "'Kony 2012' Prompts Outrage In Uganda, Future Screenings Canceled (VIDEO)," *The Huffington Post,* www.huffingtonpost.com/2012/03/14/kony-2012-uganda_n_1346114.html (accessed March 9, 2013).

42. Rollins, "The Ethics of Epideictic Rhetoric," 16-18.

43. Celeste M. Condit, "The Function of Epideictic: The Boston Massacre Orations as Exemplar," *Communication Quarterly* 33, no. 4 (1985): 288-90.

44. Condit, "The Function of Epideictic: The Boston Massacre Orations as Exemplar," 289.

45. Ronald C. Arnett and Pat Arneson, *Dialogic Civility in a Cynical Age: Community, Hope, and Interpersonal Relationships* (Albany: SUNY Press, 1999), 7.

46. Mary M. Keys, "Aquinas's Two Pedagogies: A Reconsideration of the Relation between Law and Moral Virtue," *American Journal of Political Science,* 45, no. 3 (2001): 527-28.

47. Thomas B. Ferrell, *Norms of Rhetorical Culture* (New Haven: Yale University Press, 1993), 132.

48. Cicero, *De Oratore,* David Mankin, trans. (New York: Cambridge University Pres, 2011), 118-21.

49. Cicero, *De Oratore*, 120-21.

50. Cicero, *De Oratore*, 123-25.

51. Cicero, *De Oratore*, 124-25.

52. Cicero, *De Oratore*, 124-25.

53. Cicero, *De Oratore*, 70.

54. Cicero, *De Oratore*, 120.

55. Cicero, *De Oratore*, 122.

56. Michael Leff, "Decorum and Rhetorical Interpretation: The Latin Humanistic Tradition and Contemporary Critical Theory," *Vichiana: rassegna di studi classici* 1, no. 3a, (1990): 122.

57. Leff, "Decorum and Rhetorical Interpretation," 125.

58. Thomas Rosteck and Michael Leff, "Piety, Propriety, and Perspective: Interpretation and Application of Key Terms," in "Permanence and Change," *Western Journal of Speech Communication*, ed. Kenneth Burke 53 (1989): 328.

59. Aristotle, *On Rhetoric: A Theory of Civic Discourse*, George A. Kennedy, trans. (New York: Oxford University Press, 2007), 62-63.

60. Cicero, *De Inventione*, C.D. Yonge trans., *Peitho's Web*, http://www.classicpersuasion.org/pw/Cicero/dnv1-1.htm (accessed April 7, 2008).

61. James S. Baumlin, "Ciceronian Decorum and the Temporalities of Renaissance Rhetoric," in *Rhetoric and* Kairos*: Essays in History, Theory and Praxis*, ed. Phillip Sipiora and James S. Baumlin (Albany: SUNY Press, 2002), 142.

62. Baumlin, "Ciceronian Decorum and the Temporalities of Renaissance Rhetoric," 142.

63. Baumlin, "Ciceronian Decorum and the Temporalities of Renaissance Rhetoric," 142.

64. Ronald C. Arnett and Pat Arneson, *Dialogic Civility in a Cynical Age*, 6-7.

65. Leff, "Decorum and Rhetorical Interpretation,"122.

66. Leff, "Decorum and Rhetorical Interpretation," 123.

67. Leff, "Decorum and Rhetorical Interpretation," 107-26.

68. Certeau, Giard and Mayol, *The Practices of Everyday Life*, 11.

69. Leff, "Decorum and Rhetorical Interpretation," 118.

70.Baumlin, "Ciceronian Decorum and the Temporalities of Renaissance Rhetoric," 143.

71. Michael Leff, "The Habitation of Rhetoric," in *Contemporary Rhetorical Theory: A Reader*, ed. John L. Lucaites et al. (New York: Guilford Press, 1999), 62.

72. Jarrod Atchison, "The Mystic Chords of Separation: Decorum and Jefferson Davis's Resignation from the Senate," *Southern Communication Journal* 77, no. 2 (2012): 124.

73. Rosteck and Leff, "Piety, Propriety, and Perspective," 328.

74. Leff, "The Habitation of Rhetoric," 62.

Chapter 4
Social Media, IMC, and the Audience

A rhetorical approach to social media and IMC must address the issue of audience since a hallmark of rhetoric is audience adaptability. Aristotle spoke of the importance of audience throughout the *Rhetoric*; introducing the three divisions of rhetoric, he states "of the three elements in speechmaking—speaker, subject, and person addressed—it is the last one, the hearer, that determines the speech's end and object."[1]

His advice on using maxims, for example, clearly states the suitable audience for this type of argument: "The use of Maxims is appropriate only to elderly men, and in handling subjects in which the speaker is experienced. For a young man to use them is—like telling stories—unbecoming, to use them in handling things in which one has no experience is silly and ill-bred."[2] Aristotle especially considers the audience in his explanation of enthymeme, which relies on the shared knowledge of the audience and the speaker to establish an effective argument. Cicero also emphasized the primacy of audience when he defined the three aims of rhetoric: to teach, delight, and move. The Five Canons do not work in a vacuum; they always situating the speech not for a general audience, but for a specific, local, temporal audience. The canon of invention describes the intersection of the question with the audience; the arrangement assists the audience (and the rhetor) in moving through the argument in an effective fashion; memory addresses not just the rhetor's ability to remember a speech but how the audience might find it memorable; and the delivery asks how this rhetorical artifact will be presented to the intended audience. Style, the third canon that I discussed in the last chapter, is perhaps the most audience-centric canon because it depends on the appropriateness of the message for the audience.[3]

The significance of audience in rhetoric especially emerges in IMC, which may seem like it is made to communicate with an audience.

However, a historical mass media perspective presents a more monologic communication that focused on communication *to* the audience, not *with* the audience. The roots of this are in both the history and practice of public relations and advertising. For example, P.T. Barnum's advertising efforts and press agentry tactics that promoted his circus in the late nineteenth century can still be seen in promotional campaigns today.[4] Scott Cutlip describes the United States in the early twentieth century as the "seedbed years" of the contemporary field of public relations because of the factors at play:

> In 25 breathtaking years from 1875 to 1900, America doubled its population, moved its people into cities, developed mass production, and spanned the nation with rail and wire communications which, in turn, brought a news form of national press associations and popular magazines . . . . The rise of powerful monopolies, concentrations of wealth and power, and the roughshod tactics of the Robber Barons would inevitably bring a strong wave of protest and demands for reforms by government. Out of the melée of opposing political forces would come the infant vocation of public relations.[5]

Public relations emerged as a response to this historical moment, when organizations realized they might achieve their goals with some kind of communication, rather than ignoring its audience.

The resulting volume of content generated by organizations, government, and the media became problematic for the American citizen. Journalist Walter Lippmann feared the overwhelming amount of information that the average person struggles to consume revealed a challenge of education as much as time and effort:

> So I have been reading some of the new standard textbooks used to teach citizenship in schools and colleges. After reading them I do not see how any one can escape the conclusion that man must have the appetite of an encyclopedist and infinite time ahead of him . . . . The author of the textbook, touching on everything, as he thinks, from city sewers to Indian opium, misses a decisive fact: the citizen gives but a little of his time to public affairs, has but a casual interest in facts and but a poor appetite for theory.[6]

A solution to this problem came from PR pioneer Edward Bernays, who believed in an educated elite that was best equipped to make decisions for the masses, and that the more complex information that was required to make a decision, the more "intelligent manipulation" is needed: "The conscious and intelligent manipulation of the organized habits and opinions of the masses is an important element in democratic society. Those who manipulate this unseen mechanism of society constitute an invisible government which is the true ruling power of our country."[7] Bernays, however, considered his public relations counselor as a"two-way" role, according to public relations historian Scott M. Cutlip. Bernays' book *Crystallizing Public Opinion* "for the first time defined the function as a two-way street, asserting that it was the job of the counsel to interpret the public to the institution as well as interpret the institution to the public[8]" One of the flaws of this perspective is that the public relations counsel is retained and paid by the client, not the public, presenting the illusion of the public relations counsel as an impartial communicator.

Marvin Olasky describes an example of the harm caused to the audience and an organization by this illusion. When U.S. Steel announced a price increase in 1962, the government and public opinion excoriated the company to the extent that U.S. Steel rescinded the price increase three days later.[9] This reaction resulted directly from a campaign by the steel industry to position itself as a public utility whose success was not only good for the company but good for society. Unfortunately, outside pressures (such as international steel competition) combined with short-sighted expansion (the industry chose to build more open hearth furnaces to boost production instead of investing in the more efficient and eventually more competitive oxygen furnace) led to a standoff between U.S. Steel, the public, and the government. U.S. Steel had to raise steel prices in order to survive; however, its rhetoric from the 1920s onward had focused on persuading the public that what was good for steel was good for society. Olasky states that "In this medieval, 'just price' conception of economics, the nation legitimately would have a large role in decided what was fair, so public relations would be essential . . . Year after year, a special section of U.S. Steel's annual report laid out the ways in which the public was being pleased."[10] This careful cultivation of public sentiment, which positioned the public and the government as steel's "partners" in success, backfired on U.S. Steel as soon as the corporation acted in what a *Fortune* magazine columnist at the time called "pure business interest."[11]

The illusion of two-way partnership with the public created by U.S. Steel's public relations efforts crumbled when its actions contradicted its speech. In this case, the institution didn't misunderstand its audience—the audience simply did not factor into U.S. Steel's decision to raise steel prices, despite previous rhetoric to the contrary. U.S. Steel underestimated its audience and overestimated the extent to which its previous communication would protect it from crisis, which cost the company and the U.S. steel industry dearly.

Understanding audience from a historical perspective again shows the complex relationships between institutions and audiences, and the effects of these relationships on communication are not new. Social media does not present unforeseen problems; rather, it offers a new variation on an old theme. Too little attention to audience can cause crisis, as the U.S. Steel example demonstrates. However, too much attention to an audience can also cause crisis, or at least the appearance of crisis. One manifestation of this excess of attention is the culture of attack.

The Culture of Attack

Eric Dezenhall details what he has termed "The Culture of Attack" as "the result of discontentment, new media that reward absolute conclusions, and declining standards of decorum in which once-repugnant forms of behavior are now accepted. Attackers are angry because they mistake opportunities with guarantees and confuse disappointment with betrayal."[12]

Eric Dezenhall is not the first to point out American confusion and misplaced anger. Robert N. Bellah et al. explains that Alexis de Tocqueville noticed a "restlessness and sadness in pursuit of the good life that is intensified, says Tocqueville, by 'the competition of all,' which in the United States replaces the aristocratic privilege of some."[13] Bellah et al. cite the later work of George M. Beard, who "popularized the term 'neurasthenia,' a generalized malaise that seemed to be affecting large numbers of 'civilized, refined, and educated' Americans at that time."[14] Unlike the ancient Greek spectators of tragedy, however, we have no catharsis in which to expunge this restlessness.[15] Tocqueville also observed that Americans see small inequalities more because the large inequalities have been demolished.[16] We have unlimited expectations accompanied by routine cynicism resulting from these unmet high expectations.[17] Cynicism and emotivism (believing that every moral decision is based on personal preference) are two characteristics of the postmodern moment.[18]

Dezenhall[19] maintains that this disappointment, combined with lack of shame and no sense of proportion, contributes to the culture of attack. A sense of entitlement flourished after World War II and has tainted the public's ability to understand what poverty, tragedy, and helplessness truly looks like: "Every human rights violation becomes another Holocaust; every military flare-up is another Vietnam; every breach of ethics is another Watergate; and every corporate foul-up becomes another Bhopal."[20] Lack of attentiveness to *this* historical moment leads to more routine cynicism and results in this distorted view: "Viewing a situation 'out of context' by interpreting meaning through an inappropriate historical framework fuels the flames of routine cynicism by setting unattainable expectations in motion."[21] These historical and cultural shifts have brought us to a time of communication anxiety that won't be calmed with any amount of Prozac. Without the setting of the ancient Greek amphitheater's performance of *Antigone* providing a communal experience where we can excise our concerns and worries, we instead experience individual anxiety over not accomplishing enough that cannot be expressed publicly.[22] This communicative anxiety then propels us into a culture of attack.

One way to understand those who perpetuate the culture of attack is to realize that attackers have become so tied to the notion of entitlement and to schadenfreude—enjoyment of another's misfortune—that when they do perceive a slight, it is not enough to rectify the situation. Instead, they must take the target "down."[23] The attackers demonstrate these characteristics in Eric Dezenhall's four stages of schadenfreude:

> During the first stage, *discovery*, the public identifies a target that seems to easily explain complicated situations. [...] Once the target is identified, it goes through a second stage, *coronation*, where it gets extraordinary attention at the expense of other things. In time, attackers realize the target isn't all that was promised. I call this stage *flaw-detection*. Once the target's flaws are known, it is savaged during the *humiliation/settling* phase, in which it is either destroyed or evaluated more critically.[24]

Ronald C. Arnett and Pat Arneson claim that this type of response is generated from a permeating unreflective cynicism that rejects any thoughtful engagement of a given situation: "We either manufacture a response that is beyond what is called for or we ignore what others say as we offer our attributed "real" answer of depth and insight. [...] Persons are able to convince themselves about the reality of something that, in actuality, never happened."[25]

Eric Dezenhall argues that attackers thrive on a facile version of understanding. A conventional public relations practice response would be *more* communication; the attackers just need better information and the attack will cease. However, this simplistic view of understanding (if the person who attacks me really understood me, he wouldn't be attacking me) is no longer valid. Instead, "in order for a message to be communicated, it has to be received. Attackers aren't receiving, they're attacking.[. . .] It's not a war on the haves by the have-nots; it's a war on the haves by the want-mores."[26] The only response to the attacks, which Dezenhall claims are not forms of communication but forms of aggression, is dissuasion.[27]

Dissuasion, as Eric Dezenhall defines it, is not a technique. "Dissuasion asks not why you were targeted but why *shouldn't* you be? It rejects the core belief that all grievances are equal; that all attacks are noble; and that attackers and their surrogates have a rights to your demise."[28] By advocating dissuasion, Dezenhall is saying that instead of ignoring an attack and hoping it goes away, or by thinking that dignifying the attack with a response will only fan the flames, a target must meet the attacker head-on with provable public evidence. If the target is actually in the wrong, then the target must rectify the situation and make restitution. However, this does not include falling on your sword to appease your attackers. Thus, dissuasion might be considered epideictic rhetoric, since it uncovers the real circumstances or a disclosure of wrongs with intention to right them, or as Rosenfield calls *alaetheia*—"the unconcealment of things in their 'thisness.'"[29]

Dissuasion is not necessarily a dialogic approach, or even a purely communicative approach. Dezenhall states, "Dissuasion is different from *per*suasion, which means to get someone *to* do something (and be happy about it), the traditional role of public relations."[30] Dissuasion makes attackers reconsider attacks after weighing risk associated with menacing the target and defuses future attacks in fear of future risk. Instead of persuasion, which ideally motivates an audience to action, dissuasion motivates an audience to *in*action. Most attackers are swayed by pathos, not logos, and dissuasion keeps the argument in the realm of pathos.[31]

Eric Dezenhall stated that the war is on the haves by the want-mores.[32] Another characteristic of the culture of attack is the war on those whom the attackers perceive have more and know more. Attackers are afraid of *Bildung*, described by Hans-Georg Gadamer as "the concept of *self-formation, education,* or *cultivation.*"[33] The culture of attack does not value a liberal arts education or knowledge of history and philosophy. The culture of attack has a short memory except when it comes to perceived slights and injuries. A thoughtful, educated, informed dialogue will not stop an attacker. In the age of the sound bite and sharp editing, some audiences value the speaker who can entertain in two minutes or less. The culture of attack is suspicious of *Bildung* because it plays into feelings of entitlement. The culture of attack relies on a perception of equality that claims everyone is entitled to what everyone else has. Misinterpreting the Declaration of Independence as an entitlement to happiness and not the *pursuit* of happiness sows the discontentment that Eric Dezenhall credits as the origin of the culture of attack: "A few act out their misery by exchanging the pursuit of happiness for the destruction of the celebrity and the faceless big-business."[34] This potential threat from an audience inhibits productive communication since a very clear way in which the institution can protect itself is to shut down two-way communication.

However, not every crisis resulting from the culture of attack is a result of *schadenfreude* on the part of an audience. Sometimes audience reaction to organizational behavior can create another type of crisis, what W. Timothy Coombs and J. Sherry Holladay call "paracrisis."

Audience, Organizations, and Paracrisis

Coombs and Holladay define paracrisis as "a publicly visible crisis threat that charges an organization with irresponsible or unethical behavior." The Kenneth Cole Cairo tweet is an example of a paracrisis: when Kenneth Cole tweeted that the Arab Spring protests in Egypt must be about their new spring line, the Twitter response from followers was equally public and visible. Many of the social media gaffes might be called paracrises, since two characteristics of paracrisis are that it is "primarily a reputational threat" and "paracrises are on display for other stakeholders *potentially* to see."[35] Not only does paracrisis play out publicly in social media, but it can be amplified and can migrate from social media to traditional media. Coombs and Holladay explain, "A social media echo is when other people repeat a social message while crossover is when a message moves from social media to traditional/legacy media or vice versa."[36] The audience plays a different role in a paracrisis than in Dezenhall's culture of attack; the former is audience as justice-seeking while the latter is the audience as *schadenfreude*-seeking. While the rhetorical strategy in the culture of attack is dissuasion, or motivating the audience to *inaction*, the strategy in paracrisis motivates an organization to *action*. This action may include removing offending advertisements or communication or changing business practices. According to Coombs and Holladay, "Luckily most challenges revolve around social responsibility and are easily reconcilable with organizational objectives."[37]

The phenomenon of paracrisis is fascinating, and arguably a result of increased participation by organizations and audiences in social media. However, the tactics Coombs and Holladay offer as "three social media rules,"[38] while reassuring for organizations, potentially positions paracrisis response as technique. If paracrisis is mostly due to errors in corporate social responsibility that can be corrected without violating organizational objectives and can be handled by following three rules, then why don't organizations anticipate paracrises more often? A more responsive approach to paracrisis resolution that rejects technique and embraces rhetorical sensitivity and contingency might be a more fruitful, productive, and ethical response. For example, the American Red Cross experienced a paracrisis when it tweeted "Ryan found two more 4 bottle packs of Dogfish Head's Midas Touch beer. . . . when we drink we do it right #gettngslizzerd" from its official Twitter account at 11:24 p.m. on February 15, 2011. The tweet, which refers to a craft beer by Dogfish Head Ale and a hash tag that is slang for preparing to drink a good amount of alcohol, came from the Red Cross social media specialist who thought she was logged into her personal account. The response from the American Red Cross was to delete the original tweet while tweeting this response: "We've deleted the rogue tweet but rest assured the Red Cross is sober and we've confiscated the keys." In addition to the Red Cross response (which did not include firing the social media specialist), Dogfish Head Ale also tweeted in support of the Red Cross, asking people to donate and providing a link: ". . . #craftbeer @dogfishbeer fans, donate 2 @redcross 2day. Tweet with #gettngslizzerd. Donate here . . ."[39]

Is this example a paracrisis? According to the criteria, a paracrisis is a "publicly visible crisis threat" with a crisis threat being "a situation that could escalate into a crisis." It also "charges an organization with irresponsible or unethical behavior."[40] In this case, the situation could have escalated into a crisis if the tweet wasn't removed, if the Red Cross didn't give any response, or even if the social media specialist had been fired. The crisis threat was publicly visible, obviously, and although not illegal or unethical to find two four-packs of beer, when the mission of the American Red Cross is to provide true crisis and disaster response, this could be interpreted as the organization not taking its mission seriously, or worse, that it could not be trusted to carry out its mission. The

American Red Cross/Dogfish Head Ale tweet does meet the criteria of a paracrisis. However, does the American Red Cross' response demonstrate use of the three social media rules of paracrisis communication?

According to Coombs and Holladay, the three rules are:

1. Be where the action is.
2. Be there before the paracrisis appears.
3. Be redundant and sprawl (cast a wide net).[41]

"Be where the action is" means that the response to the paracrisis should occur through the social medium that was used (in this case, Twitter). The American Red Cross responded on Twitter.

"Be there before the paracrisis appears" means maintaining a social media presence, "establishing one's voice" for the audience prior to the necessity of paracrisis response.[42] The American Red Cross obviously did have an existing Twitter presence, not only because it employed a social media specialist and a social media director but because the paracrisis would not have occurred if the Red Cross hadn't had a Twitter account.

"Be redundant and sprawl (cast a wide net)" means utilizing the social media echo and the crossover effect, using social and traditional media to communicate the message. "Social media are some of the strands that comprise the web that is the Internet. Sprawl your message across this web to reach as many stakeholders as possible. However, still limit yourself to channels that will reach your target audience to avoid wasted effort."[43] The American Red Cross actually did not follow this rule. Although their "we have taken the keys" tweet was retweeted at least eighty-five times, their response did not make a concerted effort to "reach as many stakeholders as possible." Instead, they relied on their audience on Twitter to understand and communicate their clever, well-written response. The coverage of the "rogue tweet," as it was referred to in articles on *Mashable* and *The Huffington Post*, was primarily limited to online media. However, the response from Dogfish Head Ale, who promoted the mission of the American Red Cross by tweeting a donation link and interacting on Twitter with the Red Cross, does not fit neatly into this last effort. It was a serendipitous result that came from a measured response that neither under- nor overreacted.

Instead, the Red Cross' handling of the rogue tweet reflects a rhetorical response. The Red Cross responded with decorum in line with the nature of the initial communication. They used the shared and ordinary language of the audience on Twitter—especially those who might appreciate finding two random four-packs of good beer—to communicate responsibility while acknowledging the audience as adults. In turn, their audience not only excused the initial tweet but engaged in measurable behavior that supported the mission of the American Red Cross. In terms of integrated marketing communication, the American Red Cross could consider their response successful.

Audience and the Trivialization of Crisis

The two perspectives on crisis and audience—the culture of attack and paracrisis—reflect the nature of crisis in social media. To be clear, I am not referring to crisis that relates to loss of life, injury, catastrophe, or natural disaster; much has been written on crisis communication in those contexts, and social media can be a fruitful place to communicate in those times of crisis. The culture of attack and paracrisis are notable because they *simulate* crisis. A challenge for organizations is to decide whether these situations will distract audiences from the mission of an organization or focus the audience on the mission of the organization. How can organizations and audiences distinguish between these types of crisis?

One helpful explanation is that our society engages in the "trivialization of crisis," which Ronald C. Arnett attributes to Christopher Lasch and Neil Postman: "The 'trivialization of crisis' differentiates genuine crisis from the manufactured, the unnecessary. Neil Postman (1985) states that we use media to 'amuse ourselves to death.' It is possible to use feigned crises to amuse ourselves, lessening our obligation to engage in productive work."[44] Arnett says that we should not avoid conflict— that in itself is healthy—but we should be able to tell the difference between a real crisis and a trivial or fake one. The American history of individualism, highlighted by Alexis de Tocqueville and explained in *Habits of the Heart*,[45] has given rise to a therapeutic discourse that, combined with the trivialization of crisis, leads to both the culture of attack and the phenomenon of paracrisis. Unfortunately, therapeutic discourse is difficult to avoid in contemporary communication. Organizations must recognize that their communication with audiences must be rooted in commonality, not the desire to make the audience "feel better." As Arnett notes, "Public life in organizations is not described by family or friendship vocabulary . . . . Public life requires argumentative parameters larger than an individual self and one's own versions of family and friendship."[46] Organizations that use therapeutic language like "we care about the environment" articulate promises that can never be kept, leading to routine cynicism. What may offer insight for both organization and audience is what Hans-Georg Gadamer calls *Bildung*, which is related to culture but goes beyond that concept. In his description of practical *Bildung*, Gadamer recalls Hegel's understanding of practical *Bildung*,

> It is found in the moderation which limits satisfaction of one's needs and use of one's powers by a general consideration—that of health. It is found in the circumspection that, while concerned with the individual situation or business, remains open to observing what else might be necessary.[47]

To get to practical *Bildung*, Gadamer says we must have theoretical *Bildung*, which "leads beyond what man knows and experiences immediately. It consists in learning to affirm what is different from oneself and to find universal viewpoints from which one can grasp the thing, 'the objective thing in its freedom, without selfish interest.'"[48] In other words, Bildung helps us to distinguish between true and trivialized crisis; it allows us to consider multiple perspectives. Although he does not use the term *Bildung*, Arnett describes the need to differentiate between public and private lives to foster the cultivation of *Bildung*, because "only creativity enhanced by a life enriched by more than the workplace opens such a door of opportunity and change"[49] Gadamer emphasizes the necessity of distance and differentiation: "The self-awareness of working consciousness contains all the elements that make up practical *Bildung*: the distancing from the immediacy of desire, of personal need and private interest, and the exacting demand of a universal."[50] In the example of the culture of attack, the immediacy of desire is the desire to right a perceived wrong by destroying the opponent; the personal need and private interest includes fame, money, attention, and self-esteem; and the exacting demand of a universal is the orientation toward entitlement that pervades the culture of attack. Practical and theoretical *Bildung* offers a way to reframe the culture of attack and paracrises as opportunities for organizations and audiences to engage in productive discourse about what it means to participate in public life.

For Gadamer, *Bildung* relies on an historical ground. This ground goes back to humanism and Giambattista Vico, who espoused the *sensus communis*:

> According to Vico, what gives the human will its direction is not the abstract universality of reason but the concrete universality represented

by the community of a group, a people, a nation, or the whole human race. Hence developing this communal sense is of decisive importance for living.[51]

How do we understand this *sensus communis*? Gadamer and Vico argue the *sensus communis* requires the study of rhetoric. For example, in the culture of attack, *sensus communis* does not exist in the realm of "us" versus "them." One of *Nail 'Em*'s themes is that the culture of attack is actually attacking our culture. Eric Dezenhall cites William James to illustrate this point: "'Real culture lives by sympathies and admirations, not by dislikes and disdains; under all misleading wrappings it pounces unerringly upon the human core.'"[52] Giambattista Vico's perspective on education gives good reasons for the liberal arts education and permits us to understand how we can combat the culture of attack through a development of *sensus communis*.

According to Aristotle, part of what contributes to the *sensus communis* is an understanding of rhetoric. For Aristotle, rhetoric is necessary in the public sphere. Part of the democratic privilege of the Greek citizen was the right to speak on his own behalf. In the culture of attack, when targets speak on their own behalf it is a double-edged sword. If targets stay quiet, they are assumed guilty; otherwise, why wouldn't they defend themselves? On the other hand, attackers suspect defenses provided by the target, as illustrated by the example of the Salem Witch Trials. The modern-day witch hunts employ "two of Salem's most popular techniques: depicting defense as foul play (How dare you fight back!) and depicting contrary evidence as trickery (Don't go dragging evidence into this fight!)"[53] Obviously, rhetoric has a negative reputation in the culture of attack: "The culture is fond of attributing crisis survival to 'spin'—alchemy and public relations tricks that can fool all of the people all the time. I reject this thesis. 'Spin' is dead because the public knows what it is. The whole idea behind spin is to convey sincerity. Today, the media openly covers spin itself, so we're on guard and tune out."[54]

Gadamer also defended rhetoric. In "Hermeneutics of Suspicion" he states,

> Recently, it seems, some of my colleagues have been trying to 'save my soul' from such dishonest things as rhetoric! They think that hermeneutics is no noble pursuit, and that we must be suspicious of rhetoric. I had to reply that rhetoric has been the basis of our social life since Plato rejected and contradicted the flattering abuse of rhetoric by the Sophists.[55]

For Gadamer, hermeneutics is a deeper penetration of rhetoric. Aristotle's conception of rhetoric is that it is a heuresis, or a means to find out or discover. As Hauser states, "rhetoric not only refers to suasive discourse but also to a method for thinking about communication, especially its heuristic concerns for invention . . . . Invention's animus includes taking the audience's vantage point into account."[56] The culture of attack is not only the opposite of alaetheia. It is also the anti-invention—an inauthentic way of uncovering that actually leads to more covering up, without taking the audience's position into account. Martin Heidegger claims that Aristotle's *Rhetoric* "must be taken as the first systematic hermeneutic of the everydayness of Being with one another."[57] Rhetoric as Aristotle, Hauser, Gadamer, and Heidegger see it has nothing to do with "spin" and has everything to do with uncovering truth.

This union of rhetoric and hermeneutics is important. Of course rhetoric can be used as a weapon or for unethical purposes. It can be used to nefarious ends by those who are well-trained in the art. Rhetoric's bad reputation does have a basis in reality. But the union of hermeneutics and rhetoric can enable ethical communication with audiences, because understanding becomes key, as Richard Palmer describes: "A rhetoric informed by hermeneutics would not view understanding as something transparent and unproblematical to be hurried over or taken for granted in the preparation for speaking; rather, understanding would be seen as a basic component of our being-in-the-world and the matrix of our speaking."[58]

Ideally, an audience who would be interested in understanding would seek out the public sphere as a site for this orientation toward rhetoric. Gerard A. Hauser emphasizes the idea of participation in "social and political contexts and contours" in his description of a rhetorical model of a public sphere: "A *public sphere* may be defined as *a discursive space in which individuals and groups associate to discuss matters of mutual interest and, where possible, to reach a common judgment about them. It is the locus of emergence for rhetorically salient meanings.*"[59] To reach this discursive space, however, Hauser states that members of a public must have rhetorical competence or "a capacity to participate in rhetorical experiences,"[60] including interpretation, understanding, and flexibility, which are just as necessary for audiences in integrated marketing communication (as stated in chapter 2) as in social media.

Audience in the Public Sphere: An Example

A somber example comes from the University of Pittsburgh (Pitt), which in Spring of 2012 experienced a rash of bomb threats that severely disrupted the lives of students, faculty, staff, and residents of the Oakland area of Pittsburgh where Pitt is located.[61] An urban campus, Pitt is one of the largest employers in the city of Pittsburgh and has the only medical school in the city. Its campus includes multiple hospitals and the tallest academic building in the Western Hemisphere, the Cathedral of Learning, a forty-eight-story high rise that includes historic classrooms and faculty offices.

Although actual bombs were never found, the threats that lasted for over three months numbered over 100. Pitt administration and police worked with the FBI and other law enforcement agencies to pursue the perpetrators and to enhance security on campus. However, when a bomb threat is called in, the choices for administration and law enforcement are limited, and Pitt took the action of evacuating every time a threat was reported. In March, with multiple threats a day being reported, Andrew, a market intelligence analyst whose wife worked at Pitt, decided to track the threats based on the emergency notifications he would receive as an emergency contact to a Pitt employee. He recorded the threats and any information he could collect in a Google Doc, and started a blog on the Google platform called "Stop the Pitt Bomb Threats."[62] Although the university did not endorse the site, neither law enforcement nor administration asked him to take it down. At the end of April, when the bomb threats ended, Andrew wrote a review of the blog and its purpose and evolution:

> The "Stop the Pitt Bomb Threats" blog began as a low stakes intelligence analysis exercise. I never thought it would become as big as it did. After the first week of threats, I began looking online for information about all of the bomb threats to date. Even a timeline of events would be a helpful tool for an intelligence hobbyist. Unfortunately, apart from a raw count, no media outlets were tracking this data very closely. So I decided to do it myself.[63]

Andrew maintained a position of respectful inquiry throughout his time moderating the blog, calling for unity and support of Pitt administration and police. Most of his commenters followed his lead in setting the tone of the site. Many began their comments "H2P," the abbreviation for the cheer "Hail to Pitt." Any "flaming" was edited or flagged for removal, and "trolls" (the term for commenters who only want to stir up trouble) were policed by the community. A blog visitor volunteered to moderate the comments to help Andrew manage the blog. Parents and students were reading the blog and commenting on how they understood the need for Pitt to evacuate (some of the evacuations were around 4 a.m. from the high-rise residence halls) but were frustrated with lack of sleep, lack of information, and a perceived lack of control of the situation. Many students who lived off campus also used social media (such as Reddit and Facebook) to offer off-campus housing to students who lived in the residence halls so that they would not be evacuated in the middle of the night. Most of the negative feedback posted on the blog focused on the perpetrator, who received the nickname "the Threatener."[64]

Pitt did not officially sanction the site. However, the university implicitly legitimized the blog's existence by allowing it to exist while *not* acknowledging it. The site, however unofficial, served a purpose for Pitt—it allowed the exchange of information that they could not sanction, and it encouraged a community response to a community threat. The blog served as a source of information but also as a way for the Pitt community to share the narrative of a community under siege. Because of the physical threat to Pitt's infrastructure, the gathering space for Pitt's community members moved online—allowing them to be present yet safely distant simultaneously. In this way, the Stop the Pitt Bomb Threats blog served an epideictic purpose and maintained decorum for a community that shared the virtue of unity in the face of a threat of the unknown.

Organizations that unreflectively establish a presence in social media will encounter a fragmented public sphere that focuses on individualism and entitlement that emerged from the rejection of civic rhetoric, *Bildung*, and *sensus communis,* and the discontent bred by unattainable high expectations. Fortunately, a rhetorical understanding of social media also presumes a rhetorical orientation toward audience. A theoretical frame based on historical practices of public relations and advertising rooted in modernity may not help organizations or audiences with understanding. However, examples like the American Red Cross and the Stop the Pitt Bomb Threats blog show us that a rhetorical responsiveness to the historical moment can move us away from the trivialization of crisis, or crisis as a form of amusement, and toward a more civil public discourse.

Notes

1. Aristotle, *Rhetoric*, Trans. W.R. Roberts, *The Rhetoric and Poetics of Aristotle* (New York: Modern Library, 1954), 1358b.

2. Aristotle, *Rhetoric*, 1394a.

3. Cicero, *De Oratore*, David Mankin, trans. (New York: Cambridge University Pres, 2011), 22.

4. Scott M. Cutlip, "The Unseen Power: A Brief History of Public Relations." In *The Handbook of Strategic Public Relations & Integrated Communications*, ed. Clarke L. Caywood. (Boston: McGraw-Hill, 1997), 19.

5. Cutlip, 23.

6. Walter Lippmann, *The Phantom Public* (New Brunswick, NJ: Transaction Publishers, 1993), 200.

7. Edward L. Bernays, *Propaganda* (New York: Ig Publishing, 1928), 37.

8. Cutlip, 26.

9. Marvin N. Olasky, *Corporate Public Relations: A New Historical Perspective* (Hillsdale, NJ: Lawrence Erlbaum Associates, 1987), 103.

10. Olasky, *Corporate Public Relations*, 106.

11. Olasky, *Corporate Public Relations*, 112.

12. Eric Dezenhall, *Nail 'Em!: Confronting High-Profile Attacks on Celebrities & Businesses* (New York: Prometheus Books, 2003), 14.

13. Robert N. Bellah et al., *Habits of the Heart: Individualism and Commitment in American Life* (Los Angeles: University of California Press, 1985), 117.

14. Bellah et al., *Habits of the Heart*, 117.

15. Hans-Georg Gadamer, *Truth and Method*, trans. J. Weinsheimer and D.G. Marshall (New York: Crossroad, 2004), 128.

16. Hans-Georg Gadamer, "The Hermeneutics of Suspicion," *Man and World* 17, no. 3-4 (1984): 294.

17. Ronald C. Arnett and Pat Arneson, *Dialogic Civility in a Cynical Age* (Albany: SUNY Press, 1999), 13.

18. Alasdair C. MacIntyre, *After Virtue: A Study in Moral Theory* (Notre Dame, IN: University of Notre Dame Press, 1981), 19.

19. Denzenhall served in President Reagan's administration. He now runs his own crisis management consulting firm.

20. Dezenhall, *Nail 'Em!*, 15.

21. Dezenhall, *Nail 'Em!*, 14.

22. Gadamer, *Truth and Method*, 128.

23. Dezenhall, *Nail 'Em!*, 116.

24. Dezenhall, *Nail 'Em!*, 120.

25. Arnett and Arneson, *Dialogic Civility in a Cynical Age*, 16.

26. Dezenhall, *Nail 'Em!*, 17.

27. Dezenhall, *Nail 'Em!*, 17.

28. Dezenhall, *Nail 'Em!*, 17.

29. Rosenfield, "The Practical Celebration of Epideictic," 137-38.

30. Dezenhall, *Nail 'Em!*, 201.

31. Dezenhall, *Nail 'Em!*, 202.

32. Dezenhall, *Nail 'Em!*, 17.

33. Gadamer, *Truth and Method*, 8.

34. Dezenhall, *Nail 'Em!*, 15.

35. W. Timothy Coombs and J. Sherry Holladay, "The Paracrisis: The Challenges Created by Publicly Managing Crisis Prevention." *Public Relations Review* 38 (2012), 409.

36. Coombs and Holladay, "Paracrisis," 411.

37. Coombs and Holladay, "Paracrisis," 412.

38. Coombs and Holladay, "Paracrisis," 413.

39. Wasserman, Todd. *"Red Cross Does PR Disaster Recovery on Rogue Tweet." Mashable.* http://mashable.com/2011/02/16/red-cross-tweet/ (accessed October 25, 2011).

40. Coombs and Holladay, "Paracrisis," 409.

41. Coombs and Holladay, "Paracrisis," 413.

42. Coombs and Holladay, "Paracrisis," 413.

43. Coombs and Holladay, "Paracrisis," 414.

44. Ronald C. Arnett, "Professional Civility: Reclaiming Organizational Limits," in *Problematic Relationships in the Workplace,* eds. Janie M. Harden Fritz and Becky L. Omdahl. (New York: Peter Lang, 2006), p.233.

45. Bellah et al., *Habits of the Heart,* 36-8.

46. Arnett, "Professional Civility," p.234.

47. Gadamer, *Truth and Method,* 12.

48. Gadamer, *Truth and Method,* 19.

49. Arnett, "Professional Civility," p.236.

50. Gadamer, *Truth and Method,* 12.

51. Gadamer, *Truth and Method,* 19.

52. Dezenhall, *Nail 'Em!,* 257.

53. Dezenhall, *Nail 'Em,* 55.

54. Dezenhall, *Nail 'Em,* 16.

55. Gadamer, "Hermeneutics of Suspicion," 294.

56. Gerard A. Hauser *Vernacular Voices: The Rhetoric of Publics and Public Spheres.* (Columbia: U of South Carolina Press, 1999), p. 33.

57. Martin Heidegger, *Being and Time,* John Macquarries and Edward Robinson eds. (New York: Harper & Row, 1962), 178.

58. Richard E. Palmer, *Hermeneutics* (Evanston, IL: Northwestern University Press, 1969), 127.

59. Hauser, *Vernacular Voices,* 61.

60. Hauser, *Vernacular Voices,* 33.

61. "Final Post: Social Media Intelligence and Lessons Learned." Last modified April 27, 2012. *Stop the Pitt bomb threats.* http://stopthepittbombthreats.blogspot.com/.

62. "Final Post," *Stop the Pitt bomb threats.*

63. "Final Post," *Stop the Pitt bomb threats.*

64. "Final Post," *Stop the Pitt bomb threats.*

Chapter 5
Social Media, IMC, and Communication Ethics

One of my favorite parts of working at a public university is our mission, which encourages engagement with the citizens of our region. My service to this mission often takes the form of presenting to community organizations and groups about effective and ethical integrated marketing communication, especially in the area of social media. One of the more lively sessions was with a group of community agencies, including law enforcement and local government. What began as a morning of media training became a spirited discussion of the challenges of social media. I wished I could give my audience of experienced first responders and non-profit directors a neat list of rules that would make the communication aspects of their jobs easier, so they could focus on the work of saving lives, protecting citizens, and educating children. Unfortunately, no such list exists. Instead, we must look to communication ethics to guide our actions. This absence of hard and fast rules is necessary, however; according to Ronald C. Arnett, "Communication ethics, differentiated from philosophical ethics and codes, informs us about what is ethical, bringing and information into direct contact with persons and the historical situation."[1]

Instead of a list of rules, I helped my audience think about how we must be responsive to the historical moment and to the narrative in which we work: what works for the City of Wilmington Fire Department may not work for the New Hanover County Sheriff's Office, and so on. In postmodernity, we have no one overarching narrative to guide us as we have in previous historical moments. Instead, we have to contend with competing narratives and virtue structures.[2] How, then, do we know what is ethical and what is not?

Chapters 1 through 4 of this book have focused on the possibilities for social media theorized and practiced from a rhetorical orientation. Thinking about social media from this perspective opens up conversations about the rhetorical nature of social media in integrated marketing communication. However, the critique of rhetoric since Plato has been the unethical use of rhetoric. After all, even online communities formed around morally bankrupt positions (such as white supremacists) have established and agreed upon decorous communication for their discourse. This chapter serves to explicitly establish a ground from which a rhetorical approach can be ethically sustainable.

Walter Fisher says that the way we discern ethical behavior is through narrative fidelity, claiming, "Rationality is determined by the nature of persons as narrative beings—their inherent awareness of *narrative probability*, what constitutes a coherent story, and their constant habit of testing *narrative fidelity*, whether or not the stories they experience ring true to the stories they know to be true in their lives."[3] Arnett expands on the relationship between fidelity and veracity in communication ethics. "Fidelity calls for faithfulness to a given narrative, and veracity calls for a truthfulness that makes sense for a given situation."[4] This combination of fidelity and truthfulness helps us situate our communication in this historical moment. The implications of social media usage in and for organizations introduces questions of ethical standards, guidelines, and traditions that are contested in this age of metanarrative decline.[5]

Recognizing that we are in this time of competing narratives means we must negotiate a set of goods in our communication. According to Arnett, Fritz and Bell, a good "describes a central value or set of values manifested in communicative practices that we seek to protect and promote in our discourse together . . . the question for us is what living a 'good life' or being a 'good person' looks like in a time of narrative and virtue disagreement."[6] Understanding what competing goods might be present in the communicative practices of social media and IMC is thus more helpful than a list of rules or guidelines. Before we can examine what goods social media and IMC might protect and promote, however, looking at the possibility of any common ground—what is called a minimalist and universal ethics—will allow us to then engage in what would be a more maximalist ethics communication approach.

Minimalist and Universal Ethics

Sissela Bok is one of the foremost philosophers on minimalist universal ethics. She offers a philosophical foundation in applied ethics for communication that provides fruitful ground summarizes three: "the positive duties of mutual care and reciprocity; the negative injunctions concerning violence, deceit, and betrayal; and the norms for certain rudimentary procedures and standards for what is just."[7] From these categories, stories emerge that ultimately result in narrative. In addition, these categories are meant to be a bare minimum, pointing to a more robust ethical philosophy that can connect the particulars of a situation or a story to a larger guiding narrative. However, Bok explains that these universal values are not always accepted and that we need not provide evidence for that position: "There will always be persons who reject every moral value including the most basic ones . . . In addition while the minimalist moral values have arisen in most societies, stressing their commonality does not call for proof that no group whatsoever has survived without them."[8]

Minimalist values are ones that can be understood cross-culturally, even if they are not followed in every society. Bok provides basic criteria of minimalist values: there are few of them, they need little explanation, they start from very clear prescriptions (like "Thou shalt not kill"), they need no common basis or foundation, they are about actual human behavior, not motivations or plans, and they are not the "only values necessary for collective survival."[9] In addition, they pertain to all relationships and all levels of society, from the most intimate interpersonal relationships to governments and organizations around the world. Bok makes a very clear case that these minimalist values should not be expected to function instantly in any culture; rather, they are helpful for the development of more maximalist ethical values.

Bok then argues that maximalist ethical values expand upon the minimalist values' scope, function, language, and action; they are more nuanced, textured, and ephemeral, embellishing the minimalist value structure to deal with more complex cases. They also apply to human intentions and plans, in addition to actions and behaviors, and factor into our plans, dreams, and hopes.[10] Bok's ethical theory considers all moral questions and behavior.

Bok agrees that this common citizenship is informed by both the minimalist and maximalist ethical frameworks:

> In debates about moral issues, minimalist and maximalist perspectives
> enrich one another, providing mutually challenging and reinforcing ap-
> proaches. The minimalist approach seeks common ground, some base-
> line consensus from which to undertake and facilitate further debate.
> The maximalist approach begins, rather, by setting forth a more com-
> plete position . . . . It is when these approaches are seen as different,
> each necessary but neither one sufficient on its own, that they best
> serve debates concerning values.[11]

Given the narrative contention of postmodernity, however, we cannot make claims about a maximalist ethical position as being, in the
words of Sissela Bok, "an ideal position seen as the correct one, whether
or not it is generally shared."[12] Instead, we must offer one of many potential maximalist ethical viewpoints, which can then be considered and
evaluated against the minimalist ethical baseline.

The cultivation of public *and* private virtues counteracts emotivism
in public and private decision-making. Going back to Sissela Bok's argument that no society can exist without the assumption of truthfulness,
the private commitment to truth-telling informs the public virtue of veracity, and vice versa. Integrated marketing communication is performed
in a public space, but without a guiding corporate narrative, private individuals make communication decisions based on emotivism.

I posit that the marketplace has a responsibility for the public good
and that it can look to minimalist ethics as explained by Sissela Bok to
ground this responsibility. Bok explains that most ethical approaches
share common characteristics that fit into three categories: "the positive
duties of mutual care and reciprocity; the negative injunctions concerning violence, deceit, and betrayal; and the norms for certain rudimentary
procedures and standards for what is just."[13] For example, if a company
announces corporate social responsibility in its mission statement but its
actions are not aligned with this aspect of its mission statement, then this
could be construed as deception of shareholders, employees, customers,
and the public, therefore violating Bok's second category of ethical baselines. It is necessary to understand that Bok's description of minimalist
ethics provides a ground from which a more robust understanding of ethics and responsibility can grow. Bok reminds us of this in *Common Values:*

> While necessary, minimalist values are nowhere near sufficient for a
> good life, for being in full touch with one's humanity, for a thriving
> family or community. Rather, they represent the minimum of what we

can ask of ourselves and of what we owe to others, but not in any way all that we might owe to, or ask of, those who stand in special relations to us, such as our family members, friends, colleagues, clients, or political representatives; nor all that we might aspire to in terms of the respect due to all human beings, ourselves included.[14]

Sissela Bok's third category maintains that within every society there is a system of justice to deal with violations of the positive and negative laws. This category provides for a framework for victims of violators of the positive and negative laws (or those wrongly accused) to seek justice.[15]

Sissela Bok makes no claim that all people recognize these moral values automatically; rather, she envisions minimalist ethics as "a basis on which to build negotiation and dialogue about how to extend the scope within which they are honored. In turn, they also provide criteria and a broadly comprehensive language for critique of existing practices."[16] In *Common Values*, Bok suggests some areas—such as humanitarian crises—where the criteria and comprehensive language can be applied. Note that minimalist ethics does not equate with relativism nor absolutism; the term "absolute" is especially problematic in miminalist ethics when considering the historical meaning assigned to the term.

Robert Kane explains why "absolute" is so loaded; we have arrived at the point of making moral decisions on the basis of "if others can do it, why can't we?"[17] According to Kane, three points have contributed to a loss of a spiritual center: "(1) the *modern rejection of absolute values*; (2) the *reduction of the unique core of human personality* to the objective and impersonal forces of heredity, physical environment, and collective social forces; and (3) the *loss of roots*, or a sense of cultural continuity that makes of the past a source of meaning."[18] Kane claims that we avoid using "absolute value" as a term because of the Enlightenment association of absolute values, authoritarianism, and fanaticism. His solution is to seeks a middle ground between fanaticism and moral nihilism and skepticism that comes from a relativistic understanding of ethics that rejects the absolute.[19]

Minimalist Universal Ethics in the Communication Discipline

Clifford Christians offers an entrance into the problems of finding a minimalist universal ethic in the communication discipline with a discussion of "normative ethics"—a balance between ethical philosophy and actual human behavior.[20] For Christians, the ground for normative ethics is justifiability: "The principles and standards that emerge in a normative ethics are those that are justified on grounds that others do not find defective."[21] With a definition of a normative ethic in place, Christians claims, communication scholars and practitioners can move toward finding these ground that others do not find defective. With a reference to Bok and her three questions to determine moral reasoning, Christians encourages his audience to seek a normative ethic in order to combat what he considers the driving means of suspect moral reasoning in media and communication: utilitarianism.[22]

Much of Christians' scholarship is in the area of universal ethics as a ground for communication. Christians attempts to establish a minimalist universal ethic while recognizing its limits and promoting the search for a more maximalist universal ethic. Another communication theorist, Josina Makau, also espouses a minimalist ethic through veracity and fidelity. Much like Bok and Christians, Makau is concerned about lying and deception and how these break down society. Makau's principles of veracity and fidelity offer another entrance into the communication literature on minimalist universal ethics, opposing rampant relativism with an understanding of the necessity of trust in human relations and discourse. According to Makau, "The Principles of Fidelity and Veracity derive from this recognition of the central role trust plays in healthy communication interaction. [...] The Principle of Fidelity holds that bona fide promises are to be kept. Related is the Principle of Veracity, which gives strong presumptive weight to truth-telling."[23]

Makau agrees with Bok's assessment that veracity (that lies must be explained, while truths do not need to be justified) is necessary for not only an ethical society but for any healthy society at all. In Makau's and Christians' work, the search for a minimalist universal ethics in communication must consider lying and deception because of this area's relationship to the theory and practice of communication. Integrated marketing communication does not function without a presupposition that the communicator is providing the truth. Unfortunately, cynicism (resulting from unmet high expectations) contributes to the relativist communication ethic that hampers discourse based on trust.[24]

The work of these communication scholars provide a ground for an ethical approach to social media and IMC, giving a perspective that "reasonable persons" may have cynical reactions to this practice. Veracity and fidelity offer a theoretical ground for IMC that presupposes actions that are truthful and faithful to the narrative of an organization while engaging the public trust.

Beyond Minimalist Ethics: Virtue in Communication Ethics

Beyond minimalist communication ethical standards alone, however, denies the complexity of dealing with multiple stories and narratives. While virtue ethics is not the only path toward a more maximalist ethical framework, it offers guideposts into a public story that can potentially become a corporate[25] narrative. For example, Celeste Michelle Condit argues that too much emphasis on individual virtue development forgets the public imperative of rhetoric:

> It is precisely the practice of public rhetoric that converts individual desires into something more—something carrying *moral* import, which can anchor the will of the community. This transformation of desires is possible because public rhetoric requires an individual speak a *public* language that includes linguistic *commitments* shared by all who are constituents of a community.[26]

Condit considers Alasdair MacIntyre's and Thomas Frentz's "pessimism" about anything but private cultivation of virtuous behavior unhelpful because it "privatizes public morality."[27] This pessimism occurs because "saturated with the petty lies of politicians and the grand larcenies of corporate plunderers, we find it difficult to defend moral optimism as anything other than charming naiveté."[28] In other words, this moral pessimism is much like routine cynicism resulting from unmet high expectations.[29] Condit urges us to consider the rewards of public engagement, however difficult the process or checkered the past, because it is in this community commitment that more extensive moral codes are forged beyond the bare minimum of universals: "any principle is merely a shorthand summary for the complex and objectively compelling moral imperatives that arise from the specific conditions of moral situations, including the broad, shared boundaries of the human condition."[30] While Condit offers compelling questions to consider in this time of narrative contention, her critique of MacIntyre presents the question of cultivating public and private virtues as "either/or" instead of a more fruitful "both/and."

A Virtue Ethics Approach to Social Media in IMC

Looking at social media and IMC from a communication ethics perspective means that we are negotiating the goods that we should promote or protect. I have made the argument that social media is a form of epideictic rhetoric that celebrates the everyday. Communication ethics is also not an abstraction; it is everyday engagement in the promotion and protecting of these goods. Arnett, Fritz, and Bell emphasize the everydayness of communication ethics:

> The good lives with the quality of its champions, for communication ethics does not live in the abstract, but in the give and take of life before us. We begin with a basic assumption: If you care about a given good, then showing up to engage the communicative practices of that good makes all the difference. Communication ethics does not live in codes or principles, but in the willingness of communicators to show up for the communicative task of protecting and promoting a given good.[31]

How can a rhetorical approach to social media and IMC promote ethical and reflective practice? First, I am specifically referring to an organizational context. Working from a mission-driven structure can provide answers to the questions of "should I even have an online presence" and "how would this look?" A rhetorical approach to social media situates it within the temporal, local, and particular, and is attentive to this historical moment. While quantitative measurement of visitors, page views, and other metrics are a starting point to recognizing the reach of an organization's social media presence, the rhetorical orientation of communication fleshes out a holistic picture of social media as IMC.

By reframing the discussion of social media in IMC as a form of epideictic rhetoric, which celebrates the everyday and also displays for a culture what is virtuous, a virtue ethics approach to communication ethics becomes more relevant and useful. It asks what is held as virtue—which is publicly agreed-upon, as opposed to values, which are private—and then these publicly agreed-upon virtues guide our decisions. Christians, Mark Fackler, and John P. Ferré frame community-based ethical agreements as a development of virtue ethics:

> MacIntyre advocated a new perspective on moral philosophy rooted in the way humans actually experience life and how they interpret it, that is, in community. Our common social and emotional experience help us make sound moral judgments . . . To MacIntyre, our fragmented society has no conception of the common good and no way to persuade one another about what it may be. For the communications enterprise, therefore, the shift from formal logic to community formation is appealing, and necessary for its future vitality (cf. Borden, 2007). In making this shift, virtue, duty, and consequences do not disappear from the ethics agenda. They are fundamental components of the moral life.[32]

Christians, Fackler, and Ferré call this type of ethics negotiated by community communitarian ethics. Online, which community might negotiate these ethics? This book specifically addresss IMC and social media, or how organizations and their audiences communicate through social media. So a community might be a micro-community that forms around an online media outlet: commenters on a website like Deadspin[33], an irreverent sports blog that in 2013 broke the Manti T'eo story, or the community forum on the Chronicle of Higher Education website. Recall the idea of decorum. Some language that is decorous for Deadspin commenters is banned by the Chronicle forum. At first glance, the Deadspin commenters are a crude bunch, to put it mildly. However, a careful read through comments, especially from those who have created avatars and permanent user names, as opposed to temporary "burner" accounts, demonstrates a commitment to decorum that is agreed-upon by the commenters and the regular writers. This is persuasive enough to the regular commenters that any violators of this decorum are censured by the regular commenters. Decorum in this case is not "propriety" (the language is colorful and the content often gross humor) but is a yardstick of appropriate behavior. Reading Deadspin is not for the easily offended, but it reminds us that we are not the audience for most of the content published online, as Clay Shirky asserts:

> We misread these seemingly inane posts because we're so unused to seeing written material in public that isn't intended for us. The people posting messages to one another in small groups are doing a different kind of communi-

cating than people posting messages for hundreds or thousands of persons
to read . . . . An audience isn't just a big community; it can be more anony-
mous, with many fewer ties among users. A community isn't just a small
audience either; it has a social density that audiences lack.[34]

These audiences and communities maintain a level of decorum that
works for their forum, blog, Twitter account, or web site. Acknowledging decorum as contextual from online community to online community,
allows us an entrance into constructive questions, such as: How do we
engage in decorum as consumers? How can organizations establish decorum congruent with its mission? Can the idea that we are not the audience for most of the content published online be an opportunity for rhetorical decorum? How do we seek decorum in the traces of online
communication that may never be fully erased? A virtue ethics perspective in social media and IMC encourages the cultivation of *phronesis* to
deal with this uncertainty in a productive fashion.

In chapter 3, I referred to practical wisdom, or *phronesis*, as a fundamental building block of the rhetorical tradition and of communication
ethics. The Aristotelian virtue of prudence also refers to "the virtues of
choosing and acting upon what is good according to right reason in a
specific situation amid all the complexities and competing claims of daily existence."[35] Aristotle defines rhetoric as "the faculty of observing in
any given case the available means of persuasion. This is not a function
of any other art."[36] Aquinas says the following about the relationship between art and prudence:

> The Philosopher says that there is a virtue of art, because art does not
> require rectitude of the appetite; wherefore in order that a man may
> make right use of his art, he needs to have a virtue which will rectify
> his appetite. Prudence however has nothing to do with the matter of art,
> because art is both directed to a particular end, and has fixed means of
> obtaining that end. And yet, by a kind of comparison, a man may be
> said to act prudently in matters of art. Moreover in certain arts, on ac-
> count of the uncertainty of the means for obtaining the end, there is
> need for counsel.[37]

Therefore, if prudence is necessary in those arts (like rhetoric) where
the means to an end, while fixed, are uncertain, then the virtue of prudence can inform the art of rhetoric. According to Daniel Mark Nelson,
"Art does not perfect the artisan as a moral agent . . . . Authentic prudence presupposes a good will."[38] This position establishes a connection

between the virtue of prudence and the art of rhetoric, since prudence (*phronesis*) must be present for virtuous rhetoric.

Virtue, rhetoric, and *phronesis* come together in the *phronimos*:

> Only skilled arguers—those who understand syllogisms and induction and who are knowledgeable in relevant subject matters— can frame such proofs. Moreover, they have to frame them in a way that shows discernment and good judgment on matters of practical conduct. For Aristotle, the rhetorically potent person possesses both the capacity to make—a productive capacity—and also *phronesis,* since affairs of rhetorical interest are ones determining right conduct in practical life. Such a person teaches the right course of action in the given case. This is the rhetor of whom Aristotle speaks.[39]

Therefore, a virtuous person (who must also be imbued with practical wisdom) can deliberate and decide on a wise course of action through rhetoric that is in line with the virtues.

The rhetorical tradition also includes *phronesis*, which, according to Christopher Lyle Johnstone, is "a practical discourse tradition . . . that seeks to mediate between universal truths and the concrete situation."[40] This mediator role so embedded in rhetoric is one that also begets a virtuous orientation to rhetoric and communication through *logos* (reason), which Johnstone identifies as "the foundation of moral virtue; and moral virtue emerges as the perfection of human nature . . . the exercise of practical wisdom (*phronesis)* in choosing conduct manifests the human capacity for deliberation and self-conscious action. It manifests, in short, the essentially human power of *logos.*"[41] Clifford Christians also explains the Aristotelian *phronesis* is moral insight and a type of knowledge that is neither theoretical nor technical: "making a moral decision, Aristotle argues, entails doing the appropriate action, in the right amount, and with proper timing."[42] For Aristotle, moral universals are connected to humans and their practices: "Aristotle's theory of rhetoric is grounded in and guided by the ethical principles developed in his moral theory. The proper practice of rhetoric is intrinsically ethical because the nature and function of the art are conceived against the background of Aristotle's ethical theory. He links the two arts intimately."[43] According to James A. Herrick, "Rhetorical virtues, it is argued, are discovered by examining the goods inherent to rhetoric, as well as the sources of cooperation and the standards of excellence implied by the practice of rhetoric."[44] Fisher's explanation of his narrative paradigm, after he outlines the history of dialogue, dialectic, and logic, begins, "I propose the narrative paradigm as a philosophy of reason, value, and action."[45] Bringing the idea of communication ethics into rhetoric's realm of the particular reflects Johnstone's explanation of moral virtue, which "centering as it does upon the power of deliberation and reasoned choice, provides for fundamental connections between ethics and rhetoric."[46]

A rhetorical approach to social media and IMC encourages phronesis developed by engaging in deliberation and reasoned choice; in some cases, organizations can foster the formation of *phronesis* among their audiences, and in other cases, communities can promote the development of *phronesis* through communication with organizations. The responsibility of *phronesis* falls on both parties in the communicative relationship. With this in mind, looking at how certain audiences and organizations promote and protect their sometime competing goods can help to support the ongoing development of *phronesis*—and an excellent example of these audiences and institutions is found in higher education.

An Example of Competing Goods: IMC and Social Media in Higher Education

The challenges for U.S. higher education in the twenty-first century require working from a constructive hermeneutic to integrated marketing communication that situates us in the historical moment while being attentive to the story of an organization, and in the case of higher education, an entire "industry." A story can become a narrative, according to Arnett and Arneson, if they are publicly agreed upon by the participants in a community.[47] A narrative cannot be forced upon an organization by leadership; rather, it is created by the shared history and actions of the organization. Arnett and Arneson warn of the danger of clinging to dead narratives, because they "no longer successfully guide contemporary action; they seek to confine reality."[48]

James Twitchell points out that the narrative of higher education in the United States has transformed in his critique of the university as "College, Inc." From Twitchell's perspective, the increased focus on post-secondary education as a business can be traced to some specific factors, including the G.I. Bill and increased female and minority enrollment after World War II; the Carnegie classification system, the *U.S. News & World Report* rankings, more organized university advancement and development functions, the rise of college athletics, and the exponential growth of the number of full-time faculty for the past fifty years.[49] Twitchell's understanding of the historical moment comes to a head when he cites competitive branding as perpetuating the problems of higher education:

> The frenzy at the top is creating a marketing nightmare for all. That frenzy is not just caused by anxious kids and their protective parents but is abetted by admission directors at both colleges and high schools. The College Board...goes along for the ride. [. . .] and in doing so, they foster the very situation that invokes competitive branding . . . storytelling as differentiation happens when too many suppliers are producing too many interchangeable products and peddling them to an audience too eager to listen.[50]

Twitchell's cynicism toward the stories of higher education can, as good critiques do, set us on the path of inquiry into the complex world of the branding of higher education. It is tempting to fall into in the unreflective routine cynicism that Arnett and Arneson describe as characterizing much of public discourse today; it seems like there is too much to fix. This temptation is compounded in the relationship between the professional IMC function of the institution, engaged largely in practice, and faculty who are more engaged in research, teaching, and service. Faculty can be indifferent or openly hostile toward these professionals, while the professionals might view faculty as roadblocks instead of partners. In addition, the efforts of the professional function of marketing communication in a large, bureaucratic, decentralized organization like a college or university can often perceived one way by administration and quite differently by students, faculty, and staff.

I offer that these areas could find common ground through efforts that connect these varied constituents to the mission of the university and of higher education. The challenge of promoting the good of learning the goods of student safety, health, and development, and the good of maintaining a university's economic health are often in opposition, and IMC highlights these points of tension. For example, an ongoing issue at my own institution is how to acknowledge our coastal location as an educational asset without promoting recreation at the beach as a primary reason to apply and enroll. This is a constant negotiation for many schools, not just those in desirable geographic locations. Amenities, athletics, and student life activities are seen by some as essential to the college experience and by others as a distraction. Should we ignore location and

amenities in order to emphasize academic rigor? Or should we accentu-
ate the aesthetic appeal and amenities to recruit students and include academic rigor as an afterthought? Twitchell views colleges and universities
as participants in an ever-escalating arms race—a race that most institutions cannot afford to sit out. This ongoing tension between aesthetic
appeal and academic rigor is apparent in social media efforts to target
high school juniors and seniors. The marketing of higher education must
address students' and parents' expectations of the "total experience,"
including academic quality, a solid athletics program, plenty of quality
choices in living, eating, and entertainment on campus, and an affordable
cost. Even the usually fruitful understanding of a "both/and" instead of
an "either/or" is not helpful here, because the both/and is an even more
untenable a position to hold.

Using social media in higher education IMC goes beyond the view-
book and the static website and attempts to capitalize on an "authentic"
voice—that of the student or even the mascot. One problem with promoting the institution through these "authentic" voices is that the author or
speakers are operating within the bounds of university-sanctioned communication, so many negative experiences are never offered. The other
goes back to the goods we are protecting and promoting: what is protected and promoted when positioning a student as the social media "voice"
of an institution—authenticity? And is this even authenticity worth promoting? Andrew Potter examines the philosophical underpinnings of
"authenticity," especially as it contributes to transparency, which is what
we are trying to offer ("Hear from a REAL student about what life here
at Higher Ed. U is actually like") and finds it problematic:

> In the process, through widespread engagement with social networking sites
> and other related forms of communication, they are transforming our under-
> standing of the nature of privacy and personal information while engaging
> in what is beginning to look like a massive sociological experiment in vol-
> untary disclosure. At the same time, this cultural shift is challenging our as-
> sumptions about the authentic self, in particular the familiar Rousseauian
> fantasy about perfect transparency leading to more intimate and egalitarian
> personal relationships.[51]

Integrated marketing communication in higher education is already
fraught with tensions: between the academy and the marketplace, between higher education as a commodity and higher education as a public
good, between producing good workers and educating good citizens.
Viewing IMC in higher education as productive rather than destructive

tensions from a rhetorical perspective might look like an epideictic cele-bration: while commencement and convocation are ceremonies, the real work is done in the everyday life of the institution by students, faculty, and administration. Embracing the narrative ground at one institution while appreciating the narrative ground at another and recognizing that what is decorum at one school is not at all part of decorum at another is also a fruitful approach to IMC in higher education. The stock "students in lab coats doing research while a student plays the cello" advertisement during football games on Saturday offers a promise of higher education that can never be achieved—and really, should it be? A generic approach to higher education IMC is not ethically tenable nor is it rhetorically ef-fective. The solution is to keep being responsive to the historical moment and the narrative of the institution, and rather than being a stumbling block to rhetorical effectiveness, this can actually be its catalyst. Social media and IMC offer higher education new opportunities to engage its audiences in conversations about what goods should be protected and promoted, which, in the end, can be a more ethical and pragmatic way to communicate.

Notes

1. Ronald C. Arnett, *Dialogic Confessions: Bonhoeffer's Rhetoric of Responsibility* (Carbondale, IL: Southern Illinois University Press, 2005), 200.

2. Arnett, *Dialogic Confessions,* 30.

3. Walter R. Fisher, *Human Communication as Narration: Toward a Philosophy of Reason, Value, and Action* (Columbia: University of South Carolina Press, 1989), 64.

4. Arnett, *Dialogic Confessions,* 30.

5. Ronald C. Arnett and Pat Arneson, *Dialogic Civility in a Cynical Age* (Albany: SUNY Press, 1999) 62-3.

6. Ronald C. Arnett, Janie M. Harden Fritz, and Leeanne M. Bell, *Communication Ethics Literacy: Dialogue and Difference* (Los Angeles: Sage, 2009), 2-3.

7. Sissela Bok, *Common Values* (Columbia: University of Missouri Press, 1995), 16.

8. Bok, *Common Values,* 19.

9. Bok, *Common Values,* 18.

10. Bok, *Common Values,* 20.

11. Bok, *Common Values,* 21.

12. Bok, *Common Values,* 21.

13. Bok, *Common Values,* 16.

14. Bok, *Common Values,* 21.

15. Bok, *Common Values*, 16.

16. Bok, *Common Values*, 19.

17. Robert H. Kane, *Through the Moral Maze: Searching for Absolute Values in a Pluralistic World* (New York: Paragon House, 1994), 5.

18. Kane, *Through the Moral Maze*, 8.

19. Kane, *Through the Moral Maze*, 11.

20. Clifford G. Christians, *Ethics for Public Communication* (New York: Oxford University Press, 1979), 28.

21. Christians, *Ethics for Public Communication*, 29.

22. Christians restates Bok's three questions as follows: 1) Can you demonstrate that of all possible alternatives, this was the wisest one? 2) What arguments and principles do you use to justify your behavior and how do you handle counterarguments? 3) How will a public of reasonable persons respond?

23. Josina Makau "The Principles of Fidelity and Veracity: Guidelines for Ethical Communication." In *Conversations on Communication Ethics*. Ed. Karen Joy Greenberg,(Norwood, NJ: Ablex Publishing Corp., 1991), 115..

24. Arnett and Arneson, *Dialogic Civility in a Cynical Age*, 13.

25. "Corporate," refers not to the legal business entity but to the meaning that comes from its root word, "corpus" or body. Therefore, a corporate narrative is one that is embodied and that one can buy into. For example, a non-profit might have as its corporate narrative a social justice mission.

26. Celeste M. Condit, "Crafting Virtue: the Rhetorical Construction of Public Morality," *Quarterly Journal of Speech* 73 (1987): 82.

27. Condit, "Crafting Virtue," 87.

28. Condit, "Crafting Virtue," 87.

29. Arnett and Arneson, *Dialogic Civility in a Cynical Age*, 13.

30. Condit, "Crafting Virtue," 86.

31. Arnett, Fritz and Bell, 6.

32. Clifford G. Christians. Mark Fackler, and John P. Ferré, *Ethics for Public Communication: Defining Moments in Media History* (New York: Oxford University Press, 2012), xv.

33. www.deadspin.com

34. Clay Shirky, *Here Comes Everybody* (New York: Penguin, 2008), 85.

35. Michael Keating, "The Strange Case of the Self-Dwarfing Man: Modernity Magnanimity, and Thomas Aquinas," *Logos: A Journal of Catholic Thought and Culture* no. 4 (2007): 61.

36. Aristotle, *Rhetoric*, Trans. W.R. Roberts, *The Rhetoric and Poetics of Aristotle* (New York: Modern Library, 1954), 25.

37. Thomas Aquinas, *Summa theologiae*, II-II, q. 47, a. 4, in *The Summa Theologica of St. Thomas Aquinas*, second revised edition, trans. Fathers of the English Dominican Province, trans. Kevin Knight, 2008, www.NewAdvent.org

38. Daniel Mark Nelson, *The Priority of Prudence: Virtue and Natural Naw in Thomas Aquinas and the Implications for Modern Ethics,* (University Park, PA: The Pennsylvania State University Press, 1992),79.

39. Gerard A. Hauser, "Aristotle on Epideictic: The Formation of Public Morality," *RSQ: Rhetoric Society Quarterly* 29, no. 1 (1999): 12.

40. Arnett, *Dialogic Confessions,* 45.

41. Christopher L. Johnstone, "An Aristotelian Trilogy: Ethics, Rhetoric, Politics, and the Search for Moral Truth," *Philosophy and Rhetoric* 13 (1980): 2.

42. Christians, *Ethics for Public Communication,* 64.

43. Johnstone, "An Aristotelian Trilogy," 11.

44. James A. Herrick, "Rhetoric, Ethics, and Virtue," *Communication Studies* 43 (1992): 134.

45. Fisher, *Human Communication as Narration,* 47.

46. Johnstone, "An Aristotelian Trilogy," 2.

47. Arnett and Arneson, *Dialogic Civility in a Cynical Age,* 7.

48. Arnett and Arneson, *Dialogic Civility in a Cynical Age,* 8.

49. James B. Twitchell, *Branded Nation: The Marketing of Megachurch, College Inc., and Museumworld* (New York: Simon & Schuster, 2004), 109-191.

50. Twitchell, 111.

51. Andrew Potter, *The Authenticity Hoax,* (New York: Harper Perennial, 2010), 151.

Conclusion

Researching and writing about social media can be very demoralizing. When I first started the book, students and colleagues would ask me for examples, and it seemed all my case studies had to do with how an organization or a brand had screwed up. Then they would ask me, "Well, does anyone do this well?" and I would come up with one or two cases that didn't seem to satisfy them as much as the crises did—the crises were cringe-worthy and obvious, while the successes were subtle.

This illustrates the dilemma of working in IMC, and really, in all of communication: the disasters are attention-grabbing while the success stories are quiet. But the true difference between the two are that the disasters, at least in social media, are short-lived, while the successes are much more substantive. Social media failures make the Huffington Post and trend on Twitter for a day. Social media successes make real differences in our communication and behavior. One of the most successful social media and IMC occasions, according to the ideas I have argued in this book, came recently from the combination of a hit TV show and a little-known medical foundation, and it continues to resonate.

Downton Abbey, a show broadcast on the BBC in the United Kingdom and then aired on PBS in the United States, neared the end of its second season with a significant level of viewership and social media engagement. The historical drama set in the early twentieth century highlights class drama in England. Episodes had already been aired in the U.K., and the Preeclampsia Foundation, a non-profit organization in the United States, knew that the upcoming episode would feature the pregnancy of a lead character, Lady Sybil. In the episode, Lady Sybil delivers her baby and then dies of eclampsia, a hypertensive disease of pregnancy that causes seizures, stroke, and sometime maternal and fetal death. The Preeclampsia Foundation released a statement after the show aired, stating

Last night, 8 million viewers were shocked when one of the show's beloved characters, Lady Sybil Crawley, died from eclampsia after giving birth. Although this fictional TV series represents life in the early 1900's, women in the United States and elsewhere still die or suffer terrible outcomes from the hypertensive disorders of pregnancy (e.g., preeclampsia, eclampsia, HELLP syndrome), leaving many viewers grieving also because of their own all-too-similar tragedies.[1]

In addition to the statement, the Preeclampsia Foundation "live-tweeted" during the show's airing on Sunday evening, providing commentary and facts about preeclampsia as events unfolded. They used the hashtag #DowntonAbbey to ensure that all tweets about the show (which viewers enthusiastically discuss on social media) would come up in searches for that hashtag. Tagging @MasterpiecePBS[2] and @MarchofDimes[3] encouraged conversation between the Twitter accounts for these two organizations. The Preeclampsia Foundation also posted updates on Facebook that pointed readers to Twitter and the live feed as well as to its website. On most accounts this opportunity for the Preeclampsia Foundation to further its mission, speak to a new audience with a mutual interest in the subject matter of preeclampsia, and highlight the work of the Foundation was a resounding success. Preeclampsia has no cure even today, and a major mission of the Preeclampsia Foundation is patient and provider education, since early diagnosis leads to the best possible outcome.

I bring up this example because it illustrates the ideas in this book that can help us understand social media: epideictic rhetoric, rhetorical decorum, and communication ethics. The epideictic rhetoric of social media uncovered the mud of everyday life: a routine Sunday night of television viewing. It shows how consideration of decorum can make even a painful subject such as preeclampsia and maternal death a relevant and timely topic of discussion for new audiences. And it demonstrates how organizations and communities can make the choice to use social media in an ethical manner that is responsive to the historical moment and narrative contention.

You have to look a bit harder to find these subtle successes; once you do, they emerge more and more, reviving our communicative hope. I hope this book contributes to a more fruitful and productive understanding of social media and integrated marketing communication.

Notes

1. The Preeclampsia Foundation, "Historical Drama Hits Home with Modern Day Health Problem," January 27, 2013, http://www.preeclampsia.org/the-news/1-latest-news/258-historical-drama-hits-home-with-modern-day-health-problem (accessed January 31, 2013).

2. @MasterpiecePBS is the Twitter account for PBS' *Masterpiece Theater*.

3. @MarchofDimes is the Twitter account for the March of Dimes, a non-profit whose mission focuses on maternal and child health.

Bibliography

"20 Year Usenet Timeline," *Google Groups.* 2011.
www.google.com/googlegroups/archive_announce_20.html (accessed October 23, 2011).

"About the Internet Archive." *Internet Archive.* 2001. httparchive.org/about/ (accessed October 23, 2011).

Agnew, Lois. "The Day Belongs to the Students: Expanding Epideictic's Civic Func tion." *Rhetoric Review* 27, no. 2 (2008): 147-64.

Anderson, Andrew. "Usenet History." *Usenet.* 1996.
http://tldp.org/LDP/nag/node256.html (accessed October 23, 2011).

Anderson, Paul. "What is Web 2.0? Ideas, technologies and implications for education." *JISC Technology and Standards Watch* (2007): 2-64.

Aquinas, Thomas. *Summa Theologiae,* II-II, q. 47, a. 4. In *The Summa Theologica of St. Thomas Aquinas,* second revised edition, translated by Fathers of the English Do minican Province, edited by Kevin Knight. 2008. www.NewAdvent.org.

Arena, Christine. *The High-Purpose Company: The TRULY Responsible (and Highly Profitable) Firms That Are Changing Business Now.* New York: Harper-Collins Publishers, 2007.

Arendt, Hannah. *The Human Condition.* Chicago: University of Chicago Press, 1998.

Aristotle. *Nichomachean Ethics.* Trans. by David Ross. Oxford: Oxford University Press, 1998.

———. *On Rhetoric: A Theory of Civic Discourse.* Trans. by George A. Kennedy. New York: Oxford University Press, 2007.

———. *The Rhetoric.* Trans. by W.R. Roberts. *The Rhetoric and Poetics of Aristotle.* New York: Modern Library, 1954.

Arnett, Ronald C. *Dialogic Confessions: Bonhoeffer's Rhetoric of Responsibility.* Car bondale, IL: Southern Illinois University Press, 2005.

———. "The Status of Communication Ethics Scholarship in Speech Communication Journals from 1915 to 1985." *Central States Speech Journal* 38 (1987): 44-61.

———. "Professional Civility: Reclaiming Organizational Limits." In *Problematic Rela tionships in the Workplace,* edited by Janie M. Harden Fritz and Becky L. Omdahl. New York: Peter Lang, 2006.

Arnett, Ronald C. and Pat Arneson. *Dialogic Civility in a Cynical Age.* Albany: SUNY Press, 1999.

Arnett, Ronald C., Pat Arneson, and Leeanne M. Bell. "Communication Ethics: The Dia logic Turn." In *Exploring Communication Ethics: Interviews with Influential Schol-*

ars in the Field, edited by Pat Arneson. New York: Peter Lang, 2007.

Arnett, Ronald C., Janie M. Harden Fritz, and Leeanne M. Bell. *Communication Ethics Literacy: Dialogue and Difference.* Los Angeles: Sage, 2009.

Atchison, Jarrod. "The Mystic Chords of Separation: Decorum and Jefferson Davis' Resignation from the Senate." *Southern Communication Journal* 77, no. 2 (2012): 124.

Baker, Sherry. "Five Baselines for Justification in Persuasion." *Journal of Mass Media Ethics* 14, no. 2 (1999): 69-81.

Barnes, Nora G. "Social Media Usage Now Ubiquitous Among U.S. Top Charities, Ahead of All Other Sectors." *UMass Dartmouth.* 2010. www.umassd.edu/cmr/studiesandresearch/socialmediatopcharities/ (accessed August 25, 2011).

Barnes, Nora G., and Ava M. Lescault. "Social Media Adoption Soars as Higher-Ed Experiments and Reevaluates its Use of New Communication Tools." *UMass Dartmouth.* 2011. www.umass.edu/media/umassdartmouth/cmr/.../higherEd.docx (accessed August 25, 2011).

Baumlin, James S. "Ciceronian Decorum and the Temporalities of Renaissance Rhetoric." In *Rhetoric and Kairos: Essays in History, Theory, and Praxis.* Edited by Phillip Sipiora and James S. Baumlin. Albany: SUNY Press, 2002.

Beale, Walter H. "Rhetorical Performative Discourse: A New Theory of Epideictic." *Philosophy and Rhetoric* 11, no. 4 (1978): 221-46. www.jstor.org/discover/10.2307/40237084?uid=3739776&uid=2&uid=4&uid=3739 256&sid=55978436013.

Bellah, Robert N. et al. *Habits of the Heart: Individualism and Commitment in American Life.* Los Angeles: University of California Press, 1985.

Berčič, Boštjan. "Protection of Personal Data and Copyrighted Material on the Web: The Cases of Google and Internet Archive." *Information & Communications Technology Law* 14, no. 1 (2005): 17-24.

Bercovici, Jeff. "Who Coined 'Social Media'? Web Pioneers Compete for Credit." *Forbes.* 2010. www.forbes.com/sites/jeffbercovici/2010/12/09/who-coined-social-media-web-pioneers-compete-for-credit/ (accessed August 25, 2011).

Bernays, Edward L. *Propaganda.* New York: Ig Publishing, 1928.

———. *Crystalizing Public Opinion.* New York: Ig Publishing, 2011.

"Better Homes and Gardens." *Pinterest.* http://pinterest.com/bhg (accessed March 7, 2013).

Bok, Sissela. *Common Values.* Columbia: Univeristy of Missouri Press, 1995.

———. *Lying: Moral choice in Public and Private Life.* New York: Vintage Books-Random House, 1989.

———. *Secrets: On the Ethics of Concealment and Revelation.* New York: Vintage Books, 1989.

Bonnett, Cara. "A Piece of Internet History." *Duke Today.* 2010. http://today.duke.edu/2010/05/usenet.html (accessed August 25, 2011).

Botan, Carl H. "A Semiotic Approach to the Internal Functioning of Public: Implications for Strategic Communication and Public Relations." *Public Relations Review* 24 no. 1 (1998): 21-44.

———. "Ethics in Strategic Communication Campaigns: The Case for a New Approach to Public Relations." *The Journal of Business Communication* 34 (1997): 188-202.

Brown, Stephen. *Postmodern Marketing.* London: Routledge, 1995.

Buber, Martin. *Knowledge of Man.* London: Allen & Unwin, 1965.

Burke, Kenneth. *A Rhetoric of Motives.* Los Angeles: University of California, 1969.

Cape, Robert W. "The Rhetoric of Politics in Cicero's Fourth Catilinarian." *The American Journal of Philology* 116, no.2 (1995): 255-77.

Capell, Kerry. "When Skittles Met Twitter." *Bloomberg Businessweek.* 2009. www.businessweek.com/managing/content/mar2009/ea2009038_020385.htm (accessed February 19, 2013).

Carr, Nicholas. "Is Google Making Us Stupid?" *The Atlantic.* 2008. www.theatlantic.com/magazine/archive/2008/07/is-google-making-us-stupid/6868/ (accessed August 25, 2011).

Caywood, Clarke L. *The Handbook of Strategic Public Relations & Integrated Communications.* New York: McGraw-Hill, 1997.

Certeau, Michael de, Luce Giard, and Pierre Mayol. *The Practices of Everyday Life, Vol. 2: Living and Cooking.* Minneapolis: University of Minnesota Press, 1998.

Chase, Jon. "Celebrating Steve Jobs: The iPod turns 10." *Entertainment Weekly.* October 28, 2011. www.ew.com/ew/article/0,,20538827,00.html (accessed August 25, 2011).

Christians, Clifford G. *Ethics for Public Communication.* New York: Oxford University Press, 1979.

Christians, Clifford G., Mark Fackler, and John P. Ferré. *Ethics for Public Communication: Defining Moments in Media History.* New York: Oxford University Press, 2012.

Christensen, Lars Thøger, and Søren Askegaard. "Corporate Identity and Corporate Image Revisited: A Semiotic Perspective." *European Journal of Marketing* 35, no. 3 (1999): 292-315.

Christensen, Lars Thøger, A. Fuat Firat, and Simon Torp. "The Organization of Integrated Communications: Toward Flexible Integration." *European Journal of Marketing* 42(2008): 423-452.

Cicero. *De Oratore.* Trans. by David Mankin. New York: Cambridge University Press, 2011.

———. *De Inventione.* Trans. by C.D. Yonge. www.classicpersuasion.org/pw/cicero/dnv1-1.htm (accessed. April 7, 2008).

Cohen, Jackie. "Tensions Rise Over Facebook Timeline." *AllFacebook.* 2012. http://allfacebook.com/facebook-timeline-mandatory_b75224 (accessed August 7, 2011).

Collins, James C., and Jerry I. Porrans. *Build to Last: Successful Habits of Visionary Companies.* New York: HarperBusiness-Harper-Collins, 1997.

Collins, Jim. *Good to Great: Why Some Companies Make the Leap...and Others Don't.* New York: Collins-HarperCollins, 2001.

———. *Why Business Thinking is Not the Answer: Good to Great and the Social Sectors. A Monograph to Accompany Good to Great.* Boulder, CO: Jim Collins, 2005.

Condit, Celeste Michelle. "Crafting Virtue: the Rhetorical Construction of Public Morality." *Quarterly Journal of Speech* 73 (1987): 79-97.

———. "The Functions of Epideictic: The Boston Massacre Orations as Exemplar." *Communication Quarterly* 33, no. 4 (1985): 284-99.

Coombs, W. Timothy and J. Sherry Holladay. "The Paracrisis: The Challenges Created by Publicly Managing Crisis Prevention." *Public Relations Review* 38 (2012):408-415.

Cornelissen, Joep P. "Integrated Marketing Communications and the Language of Marketing Development." *International Journal of Advertising* 20, no. 4 (2001): 483-98.

Crable, Richard E., and Vibbert, Steven L. "Mobil's Epideictic Advocacy: 'Observations' of Prometheus-Bound." *Communication Monographs* 50 (1983): 380-94.

Crystal, David. *Language and the Internet*. New York: Cambridge University Press, 2006.

Cutlip, Scott M. "The Unseen Power: A Brief History of Public Relations." In *The Handbook of Strategic Public Relations & Integrated Communications*, edited by Clarke L. Caywood. Boston: McGraw-Hill, 1997.

Debatin, Bernhard, Jennette P. Lovejoy, Ann-Kathrin Horn, and Brittany N. Hughes. "Facebook and Online Privacy: Attitudes, Behaviors, and Unintended Consequences." *Journal of Computer-Mediated Communication* 15 (2009): 83-108.

Derrida, Jacques, and Gayatri C. Spivak. *Of Grammatology*. Baltimore: Johns Hopkins University Press, 1997.

Dezenhall, Eric. *Nail' Em!: Confronting High-Profile Attacks on Celebrities & Businesses*. New York: Prometheus Books, 2003.

DiMare, Philip C. "Writing in the Absence of the Word of God: Derrida, Christianity, and the Commentarial Tradition of Judaism." *World Communication* 27, no. 4 (1998): 5-15.

Douglas, A.E. "A Ciceronian Contribution to Rhetorical Theory." *Eranos* 55 (1957): 19-26.

Doyle, Sheelagh. "Barcelona Principles get Industry Talking." *amec.* 2010. www.amecorg.com/amec-news/news.asp?id=90 (accessed August 26, 2011).

"Edelman Trust Barometer Executive Summary." *Edelman Trust Barometer.* http://trust.edelman.com/trust-download/executive-summary/ (accessed March 8, 2013).

Edelstein, Ludwig. *Plato's Seventh Letter*. E.J. Brill: Leiden, Netherlands, 1966.

Ehrlich, Brenna. "Kenneth Cole's #Cairo Tweet Angers the Internet," *Mashable.* 2011. http://mashable.com/2011/02/03/Kenneth-cole-egypt/ (accessed March 6, 2013).

Eisenstein, Elizabeth L. *The Printing Press as an Agent of Change: Communications and Cultural Transformations in Early-modern Europe; vols. I and II*. New York: Cambridge University Press, 1980.

Ellul, Jacques. *The Humiliation of the Word*. Grand Rapids: Eerdmans, 1985.

Ewen, Stuart. "Reading Logos as Speech: Heidegger, Aristotle and Rhetorical Politics." *Philosophy and Rhetoric* 38, no. 4 (2005): 281-301.

Falls, Jason. "How Pinterest is Becoming the Next Big Thing in Social Media for Business." *Entrepreneur.* 2012. www.entrepreneur.com/article/222740 (accessed October 23, 2011).

Fantham, Elaine. "Orator 69-74." *Central States Speech Journal* 35 (1984): 123-25.

Ferrell, O.C., and Larry G. Gresham. "A Contingency Framework for Understanding Ethical Decision Making in Marketing." *Journal of Marketing* 49 (1985): 87-96.

Ferrell, O.C., Larry G. Gresham, and John Fraedrich. "A Synthesis of Ethical Decision Models for Marketing." *Journal of Macromarketing* 9 (1989): 55-64.

Ferrell, Thomas B. *Norms of Rhetorical Culture*. New Haven: Yale University Press, 1993.

Fisher, Walter R. "The Case of Public Moral Argument." *Contemporary Rhetorical Theory: a Reader*. Edited by John Louis Lucaites, Celeste Michelle Condit, and Sally Caudill. New York: The Guilford Press, 1999.

———. *Human Communication as Narration: Toward a Philosophy of Reason, Value, and Action*. Columbia: University of South Carolina Press, 1989.

Gadamer, Hans-Georg. *Truth and Method*. Trans. by J. Weinsheimer and D.G. Marshall. New York: Crossroad, 2004.

———. "The Hermeneutics of Suspicion." *Man and World* 17, no. 3-4 (1984): 294.

Geisler, Cheryl. "IText Revisited: The Continuing Interaction of Information Technology and Text." *Journal of Business and Technical Communication* 25 (2011): 251-55.

Geringer, John, and Patrick Dunnigan. "Listener Preferences and Perception of Digital versus Analog Live Concert Recording." *University of Illinois Press* no. 145 (2000): 1-13.

"Gettysburg Address—'Nicolay Copy.'" *myLOC.* http://myloc.gov/exhibitions/gettysburgaddress/exhibitionitems/pages/transcription.a spx?ex (accessed March 8, 2013).

Gilpin, Dawn. "Organizational Image Construction in a Fragmented Online Media Environment." *Journal of Public Relations Research* 22, no. 3 (2010): 265-87.

Gronstedt, Anders. *The Customer Century: Lessons from World Class Companies in Integrated Communications.* New York: Routledge, 2000.

Groom, S. Alyssa. "Integrated Marketing Communication Anticipating in the 'Age of Engage.'" *Communication Research Trends* 27, no. 4 (2008): 3-19.

Grunig, James E., and Larissa A. Grunig. "Toward a Theory of the Public Relations Behavior of Organizations: Review of a Program of Research." *Public Relations Research Annual* 1 (1989): 27-63.

Grupp, Robert W. "The Barcelona Declaration of Research Principles." *Institute for Public Relations.* 2010. www.instituteforpr.org/2010/06/the-barcelona-declaration-of-research-principles/ (accessed August 26, 2011).

Guth, David W., and Charles Marsh. *Public Relations: A Values-Based Approach.* Boston: Allyn & Bacon, 2012.

Haas, Christina, Brandon J. Carr, and Pamela Takayoshi. "Building and Maintaining Contexts in Interactive Networked Writing: An Examination of Deixis and Intertextuality in Instant Messaging." *Journal of Business and Technical Communication* 25, no. 3 (2011): 276-98.

Habermans, Jurgen. *The Structural Transformation of the Public Sphere: An Inquiry into a Category of Bourgeois Society (Studies in Contemporary German Social Thought).* Massachusetts Institute of Technology Press, 1991.

———. *Communication & Evolution.* Toronto: Beacon Press, 1979.

———. Trans. Thomas McCarthy. *The Theory of Communicative Action, Volume 1: Reason and the Rationalization of Society.* Boston: Beacon Press, 1981.

Hackley, Christopher E., and Philip J. Kitchen. "Ethical Perspectives on the Postmodern Communication Leviathan." *Journal of Business Ethics* 20, no. 1 (1999): 15-26.

Hairman, Robert. "Decorum, Power, and the Courtly Style." *Quarterly Journal of Speech* 78 (1992): 149-172.

Harpine, William D. "We Want Yer, McKinley: Epideictic Rhetoric in Songs from the 1896 Presidential Campaign." *Rhetoric Society Quarterly* 34, no. 1 (2004): 73-88.

Hauser, Gerard A. *Vernacular Voices: The Rhetoric of Publics and Public Spheres.* Columbia: University of South Carolina Press, 1999.

———. "Aristotle on Epideictic: The Formation of Public Morality." *RSQ: Rhetoric Society Quarterly* 29, no. 1 (1999): 5-23.

Heath, Robert L. "A Rhetorical Perspective on the Values of Public Relations: Crossroads and Pathways Toward Concurrence." *Journal of Public Relations Research* 12 (2000): 69-91.

———. "Management through Advocacy: Reflection Rather than Domination." *The Future of Excellence in Public Relations and Communication Management.* Edited by Elizabeth L. Toth. Mahwah, NJ: Lawrence Erlbaum Associates, 2007.

Heidegger, Martin. *Being and Time*. Trans. by John Macquarrie and Edward Robinson. New York and San Francisco: Harper & Row Publishers, Inc., 1962.

———. *History of the Concept of Time: Prolegomena* (Bloomington, IN: Indiana University Press, 1992).

———. Trans. by Parvis Emad and Kenneth Maly. *Contributions to Philosophy (From Enowing)*. Bloomington and Indianapolis: Indiana University Press, 1999.

———. Trans. by William Lovitt. *The Question Concerning Technology and Other Essays*. New York and London: Garland Publishing, 1977.

Herrick, James A. "Rhetoric, Ethics, and Virtue." *Communication Studies* 43 (1992): 133-149.

Hess, Aaron. "In Digital Remembrance: Vernacular Memory and the Rhetorical Construction of Web Memorials." *Media, Culture & Society* (2007): 813-30.

Hirschman, Elizabeth C. "Humanistic Inquiry in Marketing Research: Philosophy, Method, and Criteria." *Journal of Marketing Research* 23 (1986): 237-49.

Hogan, J. Michael and Dave Tell. "Demagoguery and Democratic Deliberation: The Search for Rules of Discursive Engagement." *Rhetoric & Public Affairs* 9, no. 3 (2006): 479-87.

Hunt, Shelby. "On Rethinking Marketing: Our Discipline, Our Practice, Our Methods." *European Journal of Marketing* 28 (1994) 13-25.

Hunt, Shelby and Scott Vitell. "A General Theory of Marketing Ethics." *Journal of Macromarketing* 6 (1986): 5-16.

Hyde, Michael J. "Searching for Perfection." In *Perspectives on Philosophy of Communication*. Edited by Pat Arneson. West Lafayette, IN: Purdue University Press, 2007.

Hyland, Drew A. "Why Plato Wrote Dialogues." *Philosophy and Rhetoric* 1, no. 1 (1968): 39.

Iacobucci, Dawn and Bobby J. Calder. *Kellogg on Integrated Marketing*. Hoboken, NJ: John Wiley & Sons, Inc., 2003.

"Infographic (Trust in Media)." *Edelman Trust Barometer*. http://trust.edelman.com/trust-download/infographic-trust-in-media/ (accessed March 8, 2013).

Israel, Shel. *Twitterville: How Businesses Can Thrive in the New Global Neighborhoods*. New York: Penguin Group, 2009.

Jacobi, Martin. "Professional Communication, Cultural Studies, and Ethics." *South Atlantic Review* 61, no. 2 (1996): 107-29.

Johnstone, Christopher Lyle. "An Aristotelian Trilogy: Ethics, Rhetoric, Politics, and the Search for Moral Truth." *Philosophy and Rhetoric* 13 (1980): 1-24.

Jonsen, Albert R. and Stephen Toulmin. *The Abuse of Casuistry: A History of Moral Reasoning*. Berkeley and Los Angeles: University of California Press, 1990.

Kane, Carolyn L., and John D. Peters. "Speaking into the iPhone: An Interview with John Durham Peters, or, Ghostly Cessation for the Digital Age." *Journal of Communication Inquiry* (2010): 119-33.

Kane, Robert H. *Through the Moral Maze: Searching for Absolute Values in a Pluralistic World*. New York: Paragon House, 1994.

Kapin, Allyson. "Will Online Social Networks Help Rebuild Skittles Brand?" *Fast Company*. 2009. www.fastcompany.com/blog/allyson-kapin/radical-tech/will-online-social-networks-help-rebuild-skittles-brand (accessed February 19, 2013).

Kaufer, David, Ananda Gunawardena, Aaron Tan, and Alexander Cheek. "Bringing Social Media to the Writing Classroom: Classroom Salon." *Journal of Business and Technical Communication* 25, no. 3 (2011): 299-321.

Keating, Michael. "The Strange Case of the Self-Dwarfing Man: Modernity Magnanimi-ty, and Thomas Aquinas." *Logos: A Journal of Catholic Thought and Culture* no. 4 (2007): 61.

Kelleher, Tom. "Conversational Voice, Communicated Commitment, and Public Rela-tions Outcomes in Interactive Online Communication." *Journal of Communication* 59 (2009): 172-88.

"Kenneth Cole Tweet Uses #Cairo to Promote Spring Collection." *The Huffington Post.* 2011. www.huffingtonpost.com/2011/02/03/Kenneth-cole-tweet-uses-c_n_818226.html (accessed March 6, 2013).

Keys, Mary M. "Aquinas' Two Pedagogies: A Reconsideration of the Relation between Law and Mortal Virtue." *American Journal of Political Science* 45, no. 3 (2001): 527-28.

Kitchen, Philip J. "The Marketing Communication—Leviathan Unveiled?" *Marketing, Intelligence and Planning* 12, no. 2 (1994): 19-25.

Kitchen, Philip J. and Patrick de Pelsmacker. *Integrated Marketing Communications: A Primer.* New York: Routledge, 2004.

Kitchen, Philip J. and Don E. Schultz. "IMC: New Horizon/False Dawn for a Market-place in Turmoil?" *Journal of Marketing Communications* 5, no.2-3 (2009): 197-204.

"'Kony 2012' Prompts Outrage In Uganda, Future Screenings Canceled (VIDEO)." *The Huffington Post.* www.huffingtonpost.com/2012/03/14/kony-2012/Uganda_n_1346114.html (accessed March 9, 2013).

Lazorchak, Butch. "Using Wayback Machine for Research." *The Signal Digital Preser-vation.* 2012. http://blogs.loc.gov/digitalpreservation/2012/10/10950 (accessed Oc-tober 23, 2011).

Leff, Michael. "Decorum and Rhetorical Interpretation: The Latin Humanistic Tradition and Contemporary Critical Theory." *Vichiana: rassegna di studi classici* 1, no. 3a (1990): 122.

———. "The Habitation of Rhetoric." *The Contemporary Rhetorical Theory: a Reader.* Edited by John Louis Lucaites, Celeste Michelle Condit, and Sally Caudill. New York: The Guilford Press, 1999.

———. "Cicero's *Pro Murena* and the Strong Case for Rhetoric." *Rhetoric & Public Affairs* 1, no. 1 (1998): 61-88.

Leggio, Jennifer. "Toeing the line between privacy and social media." *ZDNet.* 2010. www.zdnet.com/blog/feeds/toeing-the-line-between-privacy-and-social-media/2663?tag=content;siu-container (accessed October 23, 2011).

Leverette, Marc. "*Mutatis Mutandis:* Writing (After Derrida [After McLuhan {After Joyce}])." *Communication and Critical/Cultural Studies* 4, no. 4 (2007): 343-62.

Li, Charlene, and Josh Bernoff. *Groundswell: Winning in a World Transformed by Social Technologies.* Boston: Harvard Business Press, 2008.

Lippmann, Walter. *The Phantom Public.* New Brunswick, NJ: Transaction Publishers, 1993.

"Location-Aware Browsing." *Firefox.* www.mozilla.org/en-US/firefox/geolocation/ (ac-cessed October 23, 2011).

Lowe, Sid, Adrian N. Carr, Michael Thomas, and Lorraine Watkins-Mathys. "The Fourth Hermeneutic in Marketing Theory." *Marketing Theory* 5 (2005): 185-203.

MacDugall, Robert C. "Podcasting and Political Life." *American Behavioral Scientist* (2011): 714-32.

MacIntyre, Alasdair. *After Virtue.* Notre Dame: University of Notre Dame, 1999.

Makau, Josina M. "The Principles of Fidelity and Veracity: Guidelines for Ethical Communication." Conversations on Communication Ethics. Karen Joy Greenberg, ed. Norwood, NJ: Ablex Publishing Corp, 1991.

Mayhew, Leon H. *The New Public: Professional Communication and the Means of Social Influence (Cambridge Cultural Social Studies)*. New York: Cambridge University Press, 1997.

McLuhan, Marshall. *The Gutenburg Galaxy: The Making of Typographic Man*. Toronto: University of Toronto Press, 1962.

McLuhan, Marshall and Eric McLuhan. *Laws of Media: The New Science*. Toronto: University of Toronto Press, 1988.

Mearian, Lucas. "Forget Digital Tunes: Analog Music on the Upswing." *Computerworld*. 2010. www.computerworld.com/s/article/9187001/Forget_digital_tunes_ analog_music_on_the_upswing (accessed March 6, 2013).

Moran, Edward, and Rancois Gossieaux. "Marketing in a Hyper-Social World: The Tribalization of Business Study and Characteristics of Successful Online Communities." *Journal of Advertising Research* (2010): 231-39.

Morrissey, Brian. "Skittles Site Ends Extreme Social Makeover." *Ad Week.* 2010. www.adweek.com/news/technology/skittles-site-ends-extreme-social-makeover-101491 (accessed February 19, 2013).

Nahser, F. Byron. *Learning to Read the Signs*. Boston: Butterworth-Heinemann, 1997.

Neel, Jasper P. *Plato, Derrida, and Writing*. Illinois: Southern Illinois University Press, 1990.

Nelson, Daniel Mark. *The Priority of Prudence: Virtue and Natural Law in Thomas Aquinas and the Implications for Modern Ethics*. University Park, PA: The Pennsylvania State U P, 1992.

Neuhaus, Richard John. *Doing Well & Doing Good: The Challenge to the Christian Capitalist*. New York: Doubleday, 1992.

Olasky, Marvin N. *Corporate Public Relations: A New Historical Perspective*. Hillsdale, NJ: Lawrence Erlbaum Associates, Publishers, 1987.

Ong, Walter J. *Orality and Literacy*. New York: Routledge, 1982.

Palis, Courteney. "Pinterest Terms of Service Get Updated." *The Huffington Post.* 2012. www.huffingtonpost.com/2012/03/26/pinterst-terms-of-serivce-update_n_1379486.html (accessed March 6, 2013).

Palmer, Richard E. *Hermeneutics*. Evanston, IL: Northwestern University Press, 1969.

Pariser, Eli. *The Filter Bubble: How the New Personalized Web is Changing What we Read and How we Think.* New York: Penguin Group, 2011.

Pena, Walther J., and J.T. Hancock. "Effects of Geographic Dsitribution on Dominance Perceptions in Computer-Mediated Groups." *Communication Research* 34 (2007): 330.

Percy, Larry. *Strategies for Implementing Integrated Marketing Communications*. New York: McGraw-Hill, 1997.

Perpetua, Matthew. "Vinyl Sales Increase Despite Industry Slump." *RollingStone*. 2011. www.rollingstone.com/music/news/vinyl-sales/increase-despite-industry-slump-201110106 (accessed March 6, 2013).

Pimlott, Herbert. "'Eternal ephemera' or durability of 'disposable literature': The power and persistence of print in an electronic world." *Media, Culture & Society* (2011): 516-30.

Postman, Neil. *Technopoly: The Surrender of Culture to Technology*. New York: Vintage Books, 1993.

Potter, Andrew. *The Authenticity Hoax: How We Got Lost Finding Ourselves*. New York: HarperCollins, 2010.

Potts, Liza, and Dave Jones. "Contextualizing Experiences: Tracing the Relationships Between People and Technologies in the Social Web." *Journal of Business and Technical Communication* 25, no. 3 (2011): 338-58.

Poulakos, Takis. "Isocrates's Use of Narrative in the Evagoras: Epideictic Rhetoric and Moral Action." *Quarterly Journal of Speech* 73 (1987): 317-28.

Praetorius, Dean. "The Red Cross' Rogue Tweet: #gettngslizzerd On Dogfish Head's Midas Touch." *The Huffington Post*. 2011. www.huffingtonpost.com/2011/02/16/red-cross-rogue-tweet_n_824114.html (accessed October 25, 2011).

Proctor, Tony, and Philip J. Kitchen. "Communication in Postmodern Integrated Marketing." *Corporate Communications: An International Journal* 7 (2002): 144-54.

Putnam, Robert D. *Bowling Alone: The Collapse and Revival of American Community*. New York: Simon & Schuster, 2000.

"Raising awareness about over-sharing." *Please Rob Me*. 2010. http://pleaserobme.com/why (accessed October 23, 2011).

Reidenbach, R. Eric, and Donald Robin. "Some Initial Steps Toward Improving the Measurement of Ethical Evaluations of Marketing Activities." *Journal of Business Ethics* 7, no. 11 (1988): 871-79.

Rickert, Thomas. "Toward the Chora: Kristeva, Derrida, and Ulmer on Emplaced Invention." *Philosophy and Rhetoric* 40, no. 3 (2007): 251-73.

Roberts, Kathleen Glenister. "Liminality, Authority, and Value: Reported Speech in Epideictic Rhetoric." *Communication Theory* 14, no. 3 (2004): 264-84.

Rollins, Brooke. "The Ethics of Epideictic Rhetoric: Addressing the Problem of Presence through Derrida's Funeral Orations." *RSQ: Rhetoric Society Quarterly* 35, no. 1 (2005): 5-23.

Rosenfield, Lawrence W. "The Practical Celebration of Epideictic." *Rhetoric in Transition: Studies in the Nature and Uses of Rhetoric*. Edited by Eugene E. White. University Park: Pennsylvania State University Press, 1980.

Rosteck, Thomas and Michael Leff. "Piety, Propriety, and Perspective: An Interpretation and Application of Key Terms in Kenneth Burke's Permanence and Change." *Western Journal of Speech Communication* 53 (1989): 327-41.

Russell, Karen M. "When does teaching stop?" *Teaching PR*. 2011. www.teachingpr.org/teaching_pr/2011/09/when-does-teaching-stop.html (accessed March 6, 2013).

Salter, Sarah. "Storage and Privacy in the Cloud: Enduring Access to Ephemeral Messages." *Hastings Comm & Ent. L. J.* 32 (2010): 365-407.

Schultz, Don E. and Philip J. Kitchen. *Communicating Globally: An Integrated Marketing Approach*. Chicago: NTC/Contemporary Publishing Group, 2000.

Schultz, Don E., and Heidi Schultz. *IMC, The Next Generation: Five Steps for Delivering Value and Measuring Financial Returns*. New York: McGraw-Hill, 2004.

Schultz, Don E. Stanley I. Tannenbaum, and Robert F. Lauterborn. *Integrated Marketing Communications: Putting it Together and Making it Work*. Chicago: NTC Publishing Group, 1993.

Scully, Stephen. *Plato's Phaedrus*. Newburyport, MA: Focus Publishing, 2003.

Segall, Laurie. "Boozy Red Cross tweet turns into marketing bonanza for Dogfish Brewery." *CNNMoney*. 2011. http://money.cnn.com/2011/02/17/smallbusiness/ dogfish_redcross/index.htm (accessed October 25, 2011).

Self, Lois. "Rhetoric and Phronesis: the Aristotelian Ideal." *Philosophy and Rhetoric* 12 (1979): 131-45.

Shirky, Clay. *Here Comes Everybody: The Power of Organizing Without Organizations.* London: Penguin Books, 2009.

Smudde, Peter M., and Jeffrey L. Courtright. "A Holistic Approach to Stakeholder Management: A Rhetorical Foundation." *Public Relations Review* 37 (2011): 137-44.

———. "Implications on the Practice and Study of Kenneth Burke's Idea of a 'Public Relations Counsel with a Heart.'" *Communication Quarterly* 52, no. 4 (2004): 420-32.

Soffer, Oren. "'Silent Orality': Toward a Conceptualization of the Digital Oral Features in CMC and SMS Texts." *Communication Theory* 20 (2010): 387-404.

Solove, Daniel J. *Understanding Privacy.* Cambridge: Harvard University Press, 2008. Kindle edition.

———. *The Digital Person: Technology and Privacy in the Information Age.* New York: New York University Press, 2004.

Sorkin, Aaron. *The Social Network.* Directed by David Fincher. 2010. Los Angeles, Sony Pictures, DVD.

———. *The Future of Reputation: Gossip, Rumor, and Privacy on the Internet.* 2007.

Sparrow, Betsy, Jenny Liu, and Daniel M. Wegner. "Google Effects on Memory: Cognitive Consequences of Having Information at Our Fingertips." *Science* 333 (2011): 776-78.

Sproule, J. Michael. "The New Managerial Rhetoric and the Old Criticism." *Quarterly Journal of Speech* 74 (1988): 468-86.

Strate, Lance. "A Media Ecology Review." *Communication Research Trends* 23 (2004): 2-38.

———. "On the Binding Biases of Time: An Essay on General Semantics, Media Ecology, and the Past, Present and Future of the Human Species." *ETC: A Review of General Semantics* 67, no. 4: 360-88.

Sullivan, Dale L. "The Ethos of Epideictic Encounter." *Philosophy and Rhetoric* 26, no. 2 (1993): 113-33.

Sweester, Kaye D. "A Losing Strategy: The Impact of Nondisclosure in Social Media Relationships." *Journal of Public Relations Research* 22, no. 3 (2010): 288-312.

———, Kaye D., and Tom Kelleher. "A Survey of Social Media Use, Motivation and Leadership Among Public Relations Practitioners." *Public Relations Review* 37 (2011): 425-28.

Till, Brian D., Daniel Baack, and Brian Waterman. "Strategic Brand Association Maps: Developing Brand Insights." *Journal of Product & Brand Management* 20, no. 2 (2011): 92-100.

Torp, Simon. "Integrated communications: from one look to normative consistency." *Corporate Communications: An International Journal* 14 (2009): 190-206.

Trimpi, Wesley. *Muses of One Mind: The Literary Analysis of Experience and its Continuity.* Princeton: Princeton University Press, 1983.

Tulley, Christine. "IText Reconfigured: The Rise of the Podcast." *Journal of Business and Technical Communication* 25 (2011): 256-275.

Twitchell, James B. *Branded Nation: The Marketing of Megachurch, College Inc., and Museumworld.* New York: Simon & Schuster, 2004.

"Twitter Now Seeing 400 Million Tweets per Day, Increased Mobile Ad Revenue, Says CEO." *AllTwitter.* www.mediabistro.com/alltwitter/twitter-400-million-tweets (accessed March 8, 2013).

Warnick, Barbara. "Rhetorical Criticism in New Media Environments." *Rhetoric Review* 20, no. 1 (2001): 60-5.

Waskul, Dennis D. "Ekstasis and the Internet: Liminality and Computer-Mediated Communication." *New Media & Society* 7 (2005): 47-63.

Wasserman, Todd. *"Red Cross Does PR Disaster Recovery on Rogue Tweet."* *Mashable*. http://mashable.com/2011/02/16/red-cross-tweet/ (accessed October 25, 2011).

Watson, Cate. "Small stories, positioning analysis, and the doing of professional identities in learning to teach." *Narrative Inquiry* 17, no. 2 (2007): 371-89.

Weiner, Mark, Liney Arnorsdottir, Rainer Lang, and Brian G. Smith. "Isolating the Effects of Media-based Public Relations on Sales: Optimizations Through Marketing Mix Modeling." *The Institute for Public Relations Commission on PR Measurement and Evaluation* (2010): 1-16.

Wilkins, Lee and Clifford G. Christians. "Philosophy Meets the Social Sciences: The Nature of Humanity in the Public Arena." *Journal of Mass Media Ethics* 16, no. 2-3 (2001): 99-120.

Williams, Peter, and Ian Rowlands. "Information Behaviour of the Researcher of the Future." *A British Library* (2007): 1-29.

Wittel, Andreas. "Toward a Network Sociality." *Theory, Culture & Society* (2001): 51-76.

Wurzer, Wilhelm S. "Nietzsche's return to an aesthetic beginning." *Man and World* 11, no. 1-2 (1978): 59-77.

Zerba, Michelle. "The Frauds of Humanism: cicero, Machiavelli, and the Rhetoric of Imposture." *Rhetorica: A Journal of the History of Rhetoric* 22, no. 3 (2004): 215-40.

Zimmer, Michael. "'But the Data is Already Public': On the Ethics of Research in Facebook." *Ethics Information Technology* 12 (2010): 313-25.

Index

About the Author

Jeanne M. Persuit (Ph.D., Duquesne University, 2009) teaches courses in integrated marketing communication, public relations, corporate communication, rhetorical theory, and communication ethics at the University of North Carolina Wilmington. Her work has been published in *The Review of Communication*. Before returning to Duquesne University for her Ph.D., Dr. Persuit worked in integrated marketing communication in the consulting engineering field and was a marketing communications manager for a Fortune 500 manufacturing company. She has consulted on integrated marketing communication projects in higher education, non-profit organizations, human resources and software consulting, and legal and financial services. Dr. Persuit served as conference planner for the second biennial Integrated Marketing Communication Conference held at UNCW in 2013 and has taught short courses in IMC pedagogy at the Eastern Communication Association and National Communication Association Conventions.